Simple Sushi

Simple Sushi

*light and healthy sushi, miso soups,
noodle bowls and more*

RYLAND
PETERS
& SMALL

LONDON NEW YORK

Senior Designer Barbara Zuñiga
Editor Rebecca Woods
Picture Research Emily Westlake
Head of Production Patricia Harrington
Art Director Leslie Harrington
Editorial Director Julia Charles

Indexer Hilary Bird

First published in 2012
by Ryland Peters & Small
20–21 Jockey's Fields
London WC1R 4BW
and
519 Broadway, 5th Floor
New York, NY 10012

www.rylandpeters.com

10 9 8 7 6 5 4 3 2 1

Text © Nadia Arumugam, Kimiko Barber, Vatcharin
Bhumichitr, Ross Dobson, Tonia George, Nicola Graimes,
Emi Kazuko, Louise Pickford, Jennie Shapter, Fiona Smith
and Ryland Peters & Small 2012

Design and commissioned photographs
© Ryland Peters & Small 2012

ISBN 978 1 84975 216 9

A catalogue record for this book is available from
the British Library.

US Library of Congress cataloging-in-publication data
has been applied for.

Printed in China

Notes

• All spoon measurements are level unless otherwise
specified.

• Eggs are medium unless otherwise specified. Uncooked or
partly cooked eggs should not be served to the very young,
the very old, those with compromised immune systems, or
to pregnant women.

• Weights and measurements have been rounded up or down
slightly to make measuring easier.

• When a recipe calls for the grated zest of a citrus fruit, buy
unwaxed fruit and wash well before using. If you can only find
treated fruit, scrub well in warm soapy water before using.

• Ovens should be preheated to the specified temperature.
If using a fan-assisted oven, cooking times should be reduced
according to the manufacturer's instructions.

• Japanese ingredients are now widely available in larger
supermarkets, natural food stores and Asian markets.

contents

Introduction

The food of the East has become so popular in recent years – and it's no surprise. From fresh fish and soft rice that melts in the mouth, to a warming, aromatic bowl of Vietnamese pho or a crisp salad, these are dishes packed full of bold flavours and ingredients that promote well-being. They have become the healthy, convenience food of our time, with more and more restaurants serving Asian-inspired dishes popping up.

But dishes such as sushi and noodle broths are also so simple to make at home and the ingredients are becoming more widely known and available. Even if you aren't lucky enough to have an Asian supermarket nearby, most of the ingredients are now universally available online.

While noodles are the fast food of Asia – quick, instantly satisfying and wholesome – it is sushi which has really come into it's own in recent years. For so long there was a mystique surrounding sushi that prevented it being a favourite with home cooks. But the complicated techniques used in making sushi can be simplified for the home and many people are now realizing how fun it can be to prepare – and how versatile too. Sushi is perfect for so many occasions, whether it's a healthy, convenient packed-lunch box or an elegant platter to serve to dinner guests. One of the most popular styles is rolled sushi (*maki-zushi*), which is the focus of the first chapter. As soon as the process of rolling the rice has been mastered, a world of filling options becomes available.

Sushi-making utensils and ingredients

Special sushi-making utensils and authentic ingredients are beautiful and useful, and sold even in supermarkets. Many brands of nori are available pretoasted and in a variety of grades – use the best you can. Some of the recipes in this book call for only half a sheet. When this is so, cut the sheets in half from the shortest side, so you are left with the most width.

When making rolled sushi, remember that rice is easier to handle with wet hands and it is better to handle nori with dry. Keep a bowl of vinegared water (mix 60 ml/¼ cup rice vinegar into 250 ml/1 cup water) on hand to make the job easier. You can use a dish towel lined with a piece of clingfilm/plastic wrap to help roll sushi, but it is definitely worth investing in a rolling mat (*makisu*) – they are inexpensive and will make the process far easier.

Serving sushi

Traditional accompaniments for sushi are soy sauce, wasabi paste and pickled ginger, and it is often served with miso soup (recipes for which can be found in the Soup & Noodle Bowls chapter). A smear of wasabi can elevate a piece of sushi from the ordinary to something truly extraordinary.

If you do not want to add wasabi in the sushi, serve a small mound on the side, or serve the sushi with a small dish of plain soy and one of wasabi and soy mixed together. Bought wasabi varies immensely; it is possible to find paste with a high percentage of real wasabi, but many are mostly horseradish – once again, buy the best you can or make your own (see page 124).

Sushi is traditionally served immediately, but if you have to keep it for a while, wrap uncut rolls in clingfilm/plastic wrap. Keep in a cool place, but NOT in the refrigerator, which will make the rice hard and unpleasant – the vinegar in the rice will help to preserve it for a short time.

With easy to follow recipes and step-by-step instructions, you can have so much fun experimenting with a whole range of exciting combinations. Just remember, when it comes to sushi, practice really does make perfect!

sushi rolls

simple rolled sushi

Wonderful party food, nori rolls (*norimaki*) are probably the best-known sushi of all. A sheet of nori seaweed is spread with sushi rice, a line of filling put down the middle, then the sheet is rolled up into a cylinder. The cylinder is cut into sections before serving. All ingredients are available in Asian shops or larger supermarkets, as well as from online retailers.

18-cm/7-inch piece unwaxed cucumber, unpeeled

3 sheets nori seaweed

¾ quantity vinegared rice (page 119)

wasabi paste or powder

to serve

pickled ginger

extra wasabi paste

Japanese soy sauce

a sushi rolling mat

makes 36

To prepare the cucumber, cut into quarters lengthways, then cut out the seeds and cut the remainder, lengthways, into 1-cm/½-inch square matchstick lengths. You need 6 strips, each with some green skin.

Just before assembling, pass the nori over a very low gas flame or hotplate, just for a few seconds to make it crisp and bring out the flavour. Cut each sheet in half crossways.

Assemble the sushi according to the method on the following pages.

Cut each roll into 6 pieces, as shown on page 13.

Arrange on a serving plate and serve with pickled ginger, a little pile of wasabi paste and a dish of Japanese soy sauce.

step by step making simple rolls

Make the vinegared rice (*sumeshi*), prepare and assemble the ingredients, then dip your hands in the bowl of hand vinegar.

1 Put a sushi rolling mat (*makisu*) on your work surface, then put half a sheet of toasted nori seaweed on top. Take a handful of the rice (2–3 heaped tablespoons) in your hands and make into a log shape. Put the rice in the centre of the nori.

2 Using your fingers, spread it evenly all over, leaving about 1.5-cm/½-inch margin on the far side. (The rice will stick to your hands, so have a bowl of hand vinegar at the ready to dip them in as necessary.)

3 Take a small dot of wasabi paste on the end of your finger and draw a line down the middle across the rice, leaving a light green shadow on top of the rice (not too much – wasabi is very hot!).

4 Arrange 1 strip of cucumber across the rice, on top of the wasabi.

5 Pick up the mat from the near side and keep the cucumber in the centre.

1

2

3

6 Roll the mat over to meet the other side so that the rice stays inside the nori.

7 Lift the top edge of the mat. Press and roll the cylinder slightly. The join should be underneath so it will stick well (it sticks together because of the moisture in the rice). Remove the cylinder from the mat and put, join side down, in a covered flat container while you make the remaining rolls.

8 Cut each roll in half, then each half into 3, making 6 pieces. Arrange on a serving plate and serve with pickled ginger, a little pile of wasabi paste and a dish of Japanese soy sauce.

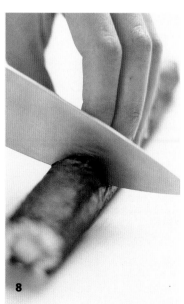

five-colour roll

Futo-maki (thick rolled) sushi are great for lunch, because they are more substantial than *hosi-maki* (thin rolled). However, they aren't ideal for fingerfood, because they are more than one mouthful.

10 g/½ oz. dry gourd*

2 teaspoons salt, for rubbing

250 ml/1 cup dashi or fish stock

2 teaspoons Japanese soy sauce

2 teaspoons mirin (sweetened Japanese rice wine)

1 teaspoon sugar

3 large eggs

a pinch of salt

2 teaspoons peanut oil

150 g/1½ cups spinach leaves, washed

3 sheets of nori

½ quantity vinegared rice (page 119)

1 small red bell pepper, halved, deseeded and cut into fine strips

1 medium carrot, grated or very thinly sliced

a 28-cm/12-inch frying pan

a sushi rolling mat

makes 24

*Gourd (kampyo or calabash) is sold dried in Japanese shops. It is a common ingredient in rolled sushi, and worth trying.

Fill a bowl with water, add the gourd, rub the salt into the gourd to wash it, then drain and rinse thoroughly. Cover the gourd with fresh water and soak for 1 hour. Drain, then put in a saucepan, cover with boiling water and cook for 5 minutes. Drain, return to the pan, then add the dashi, 1 teaspoon of the soy, 1 teaspoon of the mirin and the sugar. Bring to the boil, reduce the heat and simmer for 5 minutes. Let cool in the liquid, then drain.

Put the eggs in a bowl, add the salt and remaining soy and mirin, and mix well. Heat the oil in the frying pan over medium heat. Pour in the eggs, swirling the pan so the mixture covers the base. Cook for 2–3 minutes, gently gathering in the cooked omelette around the edges to let the uncooked egg run onto the hot pan. When the egg is set, take off the heat and fold in the 4 sides, so they meet in the middle and the omelette is now double thickness and square. Remove to a board, let cool, then slice into 3 strips.

Wipe out and reheat the pan. Add the washed but still wet spinach and cover. Cook for 1½–2 minutes until wilted. Tip into a colander and let cool for a few minutes. Using your hands, squeeze out the liquid from the spinach.

Put 1 nori sheet on a rolling mat, rough side up, and spread with one-third of the rice, leaving 3 cm/1¼ inch nori bare at the far edge. Put a strip of omelette in the middle and put one-third of the gourd, spinach, pepper and carrot, laid in lengthways strips on top.

Carefully roll up the nori in the mat, pressing the ingredients into the roll as you go. Wet the bare edge of nori and finish rolling to seal. Repeat to make 3 rolls, then cut each one into 8 pieces.

miso-marinated asparagus roll

One simple ingredient can make a perfectly elegant filling for rolled sushi. Here, fresh green asparagus is marinated in white miso.

24 small or 12 medium asparagus spears

100 g/4 oz. white miso paste

2 teaspoons mirin (sweetened Japanese rice wine)

1 teaspoon wasabi paste

3 sheets of nori, halved

½ quantity vinegared rice (page 119)

a sushi rolling mat

makes 36

Snap off any tough ends of the asparagus and discard. Bring a large saucepan of water to the boil, add the asparagus and simmer for 3–4 minutes until tender. Drain, rinse in plenty of cold water, then let cool.

If using medium-sized asparagus spears, slice each piece in half lengthways to give 24 pieces in total. Arrange all the asparagus in a shallow dish.

Put the white miso paste, mirin and wasabi paste in a small bowl and mix well. Spread evenly over the asparagus and let marinate for 2–4 hours.

When ready to assemble the rolls, carefully scrape the marinade off the asparagus – it should be fairly clean so the miso doesn't overwhelm the flavour.

Put 1 half-sheet of nori, rough side up, on the rolling mat. The long edge of the nori sheet should be towards you. Divide the rice into 6 portions. Spread 1 portion in a thin layer over the nori, leaving about 2 cm/¾ inch bare on the far edge.

Put 4 pieces of the asparagus in a line along the middle of the rice. Lift the edge of the mat closest to you and start rolling up the sushi away from you, pressing in the filling with your fingers as you roll. You may need a little water along the far edge to seal it. Repeat to make 6 rolls in all.

Using a clean, wet knife, slice each roll into 6 even pieces and serve.

inside-out avocado rolls with chives & cashews

Rolling inside-out sushi may seem a bit tricky, but it is actually very easy, because the rice on the outside moulds so well into shape, and it has the added bonus of looking spectacular.

2 small or 1 large ripe avocado

2 teaspoons freshly squeezed lemon juice

2 tablespoons Japanese mayonnaise

¼ teaspoon salt

1 teaspoon wasabi paste (optional)

75 g/3 oz. cashew nuts, pan-toasted (roasted, salted cashews work well)

a small bunch of chives

2 sheets of nori, halved

½ quantity vinegared rice (page 119)

a sushi rolling mat

makes 24

Peel the avocado and cut the flesh into small chunks. Toss in a bowl with the lemon juice, mayonnaise, salt and wasabi, if using. Mash slightly as you toss but not until mushy. Divide into 4 portions.

Chop the cashew nuts very finely and put in a bowl. Chop the chives very finely and mix with the cashew nuts. Divide into 4 portions.

Put a sheet of clingfilm/plastic wrap on the rolling mat. Put half a sheet of nori on top, rough side up, with the long edge facing you. Divide the rice into 4 portions and spread 1 portion over the nori.

Sprinkle 1 portion of the nut and chive mixture on top of the rice. Press it in gently with your fingers.

Carefully lift the whole thing up and flip it over so the rice is face down on the clingfilm/plastic wrap. Remove the sushi mat. Put 1 portion of the avocado in a line along the long edge of the nori closest to you. Carefully roll it up, then cut in half, then cut each half into 3, giving 6 pieces. Repeat to make 4 rolls, giving 24 pieces.

mushroom omelette sushi roll

Mushrooms are a very popular Japanese vegetable. Most supermarkets carry fresh shiitakes, and also may have enokis, which look like little clumps of white nails with tiny caps, and their bigger brothers, the hon-shigiri, with brown 'berets' on their heads. If unavailable, use oyster and button mushrooms.

100 g/4 oz. fresh shiitake mushrooms, about 12, stalks removed

100 g/4 oz. oyster mushrooms

50 g/2 oz. enoki mushrooms, roots trimmed

3 teaspoons peanut oil

1 tablespoon Japanese soy sauce

1 tablespoon mirin (sweetened Japanese rice wine)

2 eggs

1/4 teaspoon salt

1/2 quantity vinegared rice (page 119)

4 sheets of nori

a Japanese omelette pan or 23-cm/9-inch frying pan, preferably non-stick

a sushi rolling mat

makes 24–32

Slice the shiitake and oyster mushrooms into 1-cm/½-inch slices. Separate the enoki mushrooms into bunches of two or three.

Heat 2 teaspoons of the oil in a large frying pan and sauté the shiitake and oyster mushrooms for 2 minutes, add the enoki and stir-fry for 1½ minutes. Add the soy sauce and mirin and toss to coat. Remove from the heat and let cool. Divide into 4 portions.

Put the eggs and salt in a bowl and beat well. Heat ½ teaspoon of the oil in a frying pan. Slowly pour in half of the egg, tipping the pan to get an even coating. Cook for about 1 minute until set, roll up, remove from the pan and let cool. Repeat with the remaining egg to make a second omelette. Slice the two rolled omelettes in half lengthways.

Divide the rice into 4 portions. Put 1 nori sheet on a rolling mat, rough side up, and spread with 1 portion of rice, leaving 3 cm/1¼ inch of bare nori at the far edge. Put a strip of omelette down the middle and top with 1 portion of the mushrooms. Carefully roll up the nori in the mat, pressing the ingredients into the roll as you go. Wet the bare edge of nori and finish rolling to seal. Repeat to make 4 rolls.

Slice each roll into 6–8 pieces and serve.

grilled tofu roll

Silken tofu makes a moist, tender filling for these delicious rolls – firm tofu can be a bit tough. To make silken tofu a little firmer, put it in a bowl and cover it with boiling water before you start making the sushi.

175 g/6 oz. silken tofu

2 tablespoons Japanese soy sauce

1 tablespoon mirin (sweetened Japanese rice wine)

1 teaspoon sugar

3 sheets of nori, halved (you need 5 pieces, so you will have ½ sheet left over)

1 tablespoon white sesame seeds, toasted in a dry frying pan

1 tablespoon black sesame seeds

1 tablespoon oboro (dried pink fish flakes)

½ quantity vinegared rice (page 119)

1 teaspoon wasabi paste, plus extra to serve

a baking sheet, lined with baking parchment

a sushi rolling mat

makes 24–32

Cut the tofu into 1-cm/½-inch square strips and arrange in a shallow dish. Put the soy sauce, mirin and sugar in a small bowl or jug/pitcher and mix well. Pour the mixture evenly over the tofu and set aside to marinate for 10 minutes.

Preheat the grill/broiler. Place the tofu on the prepared baking sheet and grill/broil for 2 minutes. Turn the pieces over, brush with marinade and grill/broil for a further 2 minutes. Set aside to cool.

Cut half a sheet of nori into tiny shreds (about 3 mm/¹⁄₁₆ inch), put in a small bowl and stir in the white and black sesame seeds and oboro.

Divide the rice into 4 portions.

Spread a sheet of clingfilm/plastic wrap on top of the rolling mat. Put half a sheet of nori on this and spread with 1 portion of rice. Sprinkle with a quarter of the seed mixture, and press lightly into the rice.

Carefully lift the whole thing up and flip it over so the rice is face down on the clingfilm/plastic wrap. Arrange slices of grilled tofu along the long edge of the nori closest to you, smear with a little wasabi paste and carefully roll up. Repeat to make 4 rolls, then slice each roll into 6-8 pieces.

Serve with extra wasabi and your choice of accompaniments.

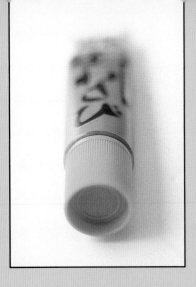

battleship sushi

Battleship sushi is individually hand rolled so the nori comes about a half centimetre/quarter inch above the rice, leaving room for less manageable toppings such as fish roe. Small cubes of different-coloured fish make a lovely topping and you don't need to be an expert fish slicer to get tender pieces. You do, however, need very fresh raw fish – that is what 'sushi- or sashimi-grade' means. If you have access to a proper Japanese fishmonger, that's perfect. Otherwise, go to a fish market, or other outlet where you can be sure the fish is ultra-fresh.

75 g/3 oz. piece of sushi-grade raw salmon

75 g/3 oz. piece of sushi-grade raw tuna

75 g/3 oz. piece of sushi-grade raw white fish (try sea bream or halibut)

½ quantity vinegared rice (page 119)

4 sheets of nori

1 teaspoon wasabi paste (optional)

1 tablespoon salmon caviar (keta)

a sushi rolling mat

makes 18

Cut the salmon, tuna and white fish into ½-cm/¼-inch cubes, put in a bowl and mix gently.

Divide the seasoned sushi rice into 18 portions, a little smaller than a table tennis ball. Gently squeeze each piece into a flattened oval shape, about 2 cm/¾ inch high. With dry hands, cut the nori sheets into 2.5-cm/1-inch strips, and wrap each piece of rice in one strip with the rough side of the nori facing inwards. Seal the ends with a dab of water. You should have about ½ cm/¼ inch of nori above the rice.

Put a dab of wasabi, if using, on top of the rice, then add a heaped teaspoon of the fish cubes, and a little salmon caviar.

sushi wraps

These wraps are best made as close to eating as possible, ideally within an hour as the nori will soften once filled. For hands-on entertaining, provide separate dishes of the individual ingredients, plus the cooked rice and nori sheets, and let everyone make their own wraps, choosing their favourite fillings

½ small avocado

1 tablespoon freshly squeezed lemon juice

½ quantity vinegared rice (see page 119)

4 sheets nori, each cut into four

2 tablespoons wasabi paste

100 g/4 oz. fresh tuna fillet, cut into 8 fingers

½ yellow bell pepper, deseeded and cut into sticks

50 g/2 oz. smoked salmon slices, cut into 8 pieces

8 cooked and shelled tiger prawns/shrimp

6-cm/2½-inch piece cucumber, cut into sticks

pickled ginger, to serve

Japanese soy sauce, to serve

makes 16

Peel the avocado and cut it into slices. Put the lemon juice in a shallow dish, add the avocado and toss to coat.

Spread 2 tablespoons of rice over a piece of nori. Add a small amount of wasabi paste and top with a piece each of tuna, pepper and avocado. You may find this easier if you hold the nori on the palm of your hand to fill. Roll up into a cone shape. Dampen the final edge with water or shoyu sauce to stick together. Fill 7 more squares of nori in the same way.

Fill the remaining nori squares with rice topped with a smoked salmon piece, a prawn/shrimp and a couple of cucumber sticks. Serve the sushi wraps with small dishes of pickled ginger and shoyu sauce.

yakitori octopus roll

Yakitori is the name given to food grilled on skewers over a charcoal fire. It can be anything – chicken, steak, liver or the octopus used here. Prawns/shrimp, scallops or any firm fish also work well. You should cook the octopus very fast over a fire to get an authentic flavour, but a hot grill/broiler will also work.

6 octopus tentacles, about 1 kg/2 lbs., tenderized, skin and suckers removed

6 spring onions/scallions

2 tablespoons sake

2 tablespoons Japanese soy sauce

1 teaspoon sugar

1 teaspoon freshly grated ginger

3 sheets of nori, halved

½ quantity vinegared rice (page 119), divided into 6 portions

5 bamboo skewers, soaked in water for 30 minutes

a sushi rolling mat

makes 30

Cut the octopus into 2.5-cm/1-inch pieces. Cut the spring onions/scallions into 2.5-cm/1-inch lengths. Thread the pieces of octopus and spring onion/scallion alternately crossways onto the soaked skewers.

Put the sake, soy, sugar and ginger into a small bowl or jug/pitcher, mix well, then pour over the octopus skewers and let marinate at room temperature for 30 minutes, turning occasionally.

Preheat a barbecue or grill/broiler to very hot. Set the yakitori skewers about 7 cm/3 inches from the heat and cook for 4–5 minutes, turning once. Remove from the heat and let cool.

Put a sheet of nori, rough side up, on a rolling mat with the long edge towards you. Top with 1 portion of the sushi rice, spread in a thin layer, leaving about 2 cm/¾ inch of bare nori on the far edge. Arrange pieces of the octopus, end to end, in a line along the middle of the rice, then put a line of spring onions/scallions on top.

Lift the edge of the mat closest to you and start rolling up the sushi away from you, pressing in the filling with your fingers as you roll. You may need a little water along the far edge to seal it. Repeat to make 6 rolls. Using a clean wet knife, slice each roll into 5 even pieces.

Note If the octopus has not been pre-tenderized, you can either beat it with a meat mallet or try this Portuguese method. Wash well and put in a large saucepan with 1 sliced onion. Cover with a lid and slowly bring to the boil over low heat (there will be enough moisture in the octopus to do this without added water). Let simmer for 30–40 minutes until tender. Cool, then pull off and discard the purple skin and suckers.

pickled salmon roll

To many sushi fans, delicious raw fish is part of the pleasure of this dish. However, if you're not an aficionado of fish *au naturel*, using smoked or pickled fish is a delicious compromise. It is very easy to pickle fish at home, and you can control the sharpness more easily.

3 sheets of nori, halved

½ quantity vinegared rice (page 119), divided into 6 portions

1 teaspoon wasabi paste (optional)

pickled salmon

100 ml/⅔ cup rice wine vinegar

2 teaspoons salt

2 tablespoons sugar

zest of 1 unwaxed lemon, removed with a lemon zester

300 g/10½ oz. salmon fillet, skinned and boned

4 shallots, finely sliced

a sushi rolling mat

makes 36–42

To prepare the salmon, put the vinegar, salt, sugar and lemon zest in a saucepan with 60 ml/¼ cup water. Bring to the boil, reduce the heat, then simmer for 3 minutes. Let cool.

Put the salmon fillet in a plastic container with the shallots. Pour the vinegar mixture over the top and cover tightly. Refrigerate for 2–3 days, turning the salmon in the pickle once a day.

When ready to make the sushi, drain the salmon and shallots. Slice the salmon as finely as possible and divide into 6 portions.

Put a half sheet of nori, rough side up, on a rolling mat with the long edge towards you. Top with 1 portion of the sushi rice and spread it out in a thin layer, leaving about 2 cm/¾ inch of bare nori at the far edge. Smear a little wasabi paste down the centre of the rice if you like. Arrange 1 portion of the salmon slices in a line along the middle of the rice and top with a line of the pickled shallots.

Lift the edge of the mat closest to you and start rolling the sushi away from you, pressing in the filling with your fingers as you roll. You may need a little water along the far edge to seal it. Repeat with the remaining ingredients to make 6 rolls. Using a clean wet knife, slice each roll into 6–7 even pieces.

wasabi mayonnaise & tuna roll

This is a rather Western idea of sushi, but it is easy and convenient because it uses canned tuna, cutting out some of the fiddly preparation of fresh fish. Use Japanese mayonnaise if you can, but homemade or good-quality bought mayonnaise works well.

4 sheets of nori

185 g/6½ oz. canned tuna in brine, drained

4 teaspoons Japanese or other mayonnaise

1 teaspoon wasabi paste, or to taste

125 g/4½ oz. baby corn, fresh or frozen, or equivalent drained canned baby corn

½ quantity vinegared rice (page 119), divided into 4 portions

a sushi rolling mat

makes 24–28

Trim a 2.5 cm/1-inch strip from one long edge of each sheet of nori and reserve for another use.

Put the tuna and mayonnaise in a bowl and stir in the wasabi.

If using fresh or frozen corn, bring a saucepan of water to the boil and cook the corn for 3 minutes, or until tender. Drain and rinse under cold water to cool. If using canned corn, drain and rinse.

Set a sheet of nori, rough side up, on a rolling mat with the long edge towards you. Top with 1 portion of the sushi rice, and spread it in a thin layer, leaving about 2 cm/¾ inch of bare nori on the far edge. Spoon a quarter of the tuna mixture in a line along the middle of the rice and top with a line of corn, set end to end.

Lift the edge of the mat closest to you and start rolling up the sushi away from you, pressing in the filling with your fingers as you roll. You may need a little water along the far edge to seal it. Repeat to make 4 rolls. Using a clean, wet knife, slice each roll into 6–7 even pieces.

teriyaki chicken roll with miso dipping sauce

Fragrant teriyaki chicken is wonderful served on its own, but can also act as the perfect filling for sushi rolls. You can buy pre-prepared teriyaki sauces or marinades, but it is well worth taking the extra time to make your own.

400 g/14 oz. boneless, skinless chicken thigh or breast (2 breasts, 4 thighs), cut into 1-cm/½-inch strips

4 sheets of nori

½ quantity vinegared rice (page 119), divided into 4 portions

1 teaspoon wasabi paste

teriyaki sauce

2 tablespoons Japanese soy sauce

2 tablespoons mirin (sweetened Japanese rice wine)

2 tablespoons chicken stock

teriyaki glaze

1 teaspoon sugar

½ teaspoon cornflour/cornstarch

miso dipping sauce

2 tablespoons white miso paste

1 tablespoon sugar

125 ml/½ cup sake

1 small egg yolk

12 bamboo skewers, soaked in water for 30 minutes

a sushi rolling mat

makes 24–28

To make the teriyaki sauce, mix the soy, mirin and chicken stock in a small saucepan and bring to the boil. Remove from the heat and let cool.

To make the teriyaki glaze, mix the sugar and cornflour/cornstarch in a small bowl with a little cold water to slacken, then stir in 2 tablespoons of the teriyaki sauce. Set aside.

Thread the strips of chicken onto the soaked skewers. Brush the chicken skewers with half the teriyaki sauce and let marinate for about 10 minutes. Preheat a grill/broiler or barbecue to very hot. Set the chicken skewers under the grill/ broiler. Grill/broil for 2–3 minutes, turn the skewers over and brush with more sauce and grill for a further 2–3 minutes until cooked. Remove from the heat, pour over the teriyaki glaze, let cool, then unthread. The chicken must be cold.

Set a sheet of nori, rough side up, on a rolling mat with the long edge towards you. Top with quarter of the sushi rice, spread in a thin layer covering about half of the nori closest to you. Put a quarter of the chicken in a line along the middle of the rice and smear with a little wasabi.

Lift the edge of the mat closest to you and start rolling up the sushi away from you, pressing in the filling with your fingers as you roll. You may need a little water along the far edge to seal it. Repeat with the remaining ingredients, to make 4 rolls. Using a clean wet knife, slice each roll into 6–7 even pieces.

To make the white miso dipping sauce, put the miso, sugar and sake in a small saucepan over medium heat and bring to a simmer, reduce the heat to low, and cook for 3 minutes, stirring constantly to stop it burning.

Remove from the heat and quickly stir in the egg yolk, strain if necessary, and let cool before serving with the sushi.

pressed &
hand-moulded sushi

Mackerel sushi pieces

Smoked fish sushi

Stars, hearts & flowers

Egg cup sushi

Stuffed squid sushi

Hand-moulded sushi

Lettuce boats

Sushi balls with roast pork & pickled plums

Marinated beef sushi

mackerel sushi pieces

Battera, a speciality from Osaka, is one of the most popular sushi in Japan. It is made in a container or moulded into a log with a sushi mat and cut into small pieces. In restaurants and shops it often comes wrapped up with a transparent sheet of kombu (dried kelp).

1 medium fresh mackerel, about 400 g/14 oz., filleted

3–4 tablespoons Japanese rice vinegar

sea salt

½ quantity vinegared rice (page 119)

pickled ginger, to serve

Japanese soy sauce, to serve

a wooden mould or rectangular plastic container, 18 x 12 x 5 cm/ 7 x 4½ x 2 inches

makes 16

Start the preparation for this dish a few hours before cooking the rice. Take a dish larger than the fish fillets and cover with a thick layer of salt. Put the mackerel fillets, flesh side down, on top of the salt and cover completely with more salt. Set aside for 3–4 hours. Remove the mackerel and rub off the salt with damp kitchen paper. Carefully remove all the bones with tweezers, then put into a dish and pour the rice vinegar over the fillets. Leave to marinate for 30 minutes.

Using your fingers, carefully remove the transparent skin from each fillet, starting at the tail end. Put the fillets, skin side down, on a cutting board and slice off the highest part from the centre of the flesh so the fillets will be fairly flat. Keep the trimmings.

Line a wet wooden mould or rectangular container with a large piece of clingfilm/plastic wrap.

Put a fillet, skin side down, in the mould or container. Fill the gaps with the other fillet and trimmings. Press the cooked rice down firmly on top of the fish (dip your fingers in hand vinegar if the rice is sticking to them). Put the wet wooden lid on top, or fold in the clingfilm/plastic wrap and put a piece of cardboard and a weight on top.

You can leave it in a cool place (not the refrigerator) for a few hours. When ready to serve, remove from the container and unwrap any clingfilm/plastic wrap. Take a very sharp knife and wipe it with a vinegar-soaked cloth or piece of kitchen paper. Cut the block of sushi in 4 lengthways, then in 4 crossways, making 16 pieces in all.

Arrange on a plate, and serve with pickled ginger and a little soy sauce in small individual dishes.

smoked fish sushi

Oshi-zushi (pressed sushi) like this, or *Bo-zushi* (log sushi) will keep for up to 36 hours – as a result, they are the best-selling items at all Japanese airports. Travellers buy them for Japanese friends living abroad as a reminder of the true taste of Japan. They are easy to make and can be made the day before.

150 g/5 oz. smoked rainbow trout or smoked salmon, thickly sliced

2 slices lemon, cut into 16 fan-shaped pieces

½ quantity vinegared rice (page 119)

pickled ginger, to serve

Japanese soy sauce, to serve

a wooden mould or rectangular plastic container, 18 x 12 x 5 cm/ 7 x 4½ x 2 inches

makes 16 pieces

Lay the trout or salmon slices evenly in the bottom of a wet wooden mould. Alternatively, use a rectangular plastic container lined with a piece of clingfilm/plastic wrap large enough for the edges to hang out of the container.

Transfer the vinegared rice into the mould and press it firmly and evenly into the mould (dip your fingers in hand vinegar if the rice is sticking to them). Put the wet wooden lid on top. If using a plastic container, fold in the clingfilm/ plastic wrap to cover the rice and top with a piece of cardboard just big enough to cover the rice, and put a weight on top. Leave in a cool place (not the refrigerator) for 2–3 hours or overnight.

When ready to serve, remove from the container and unwrap any clingfilm/ plastic wrap. Take a very sharp knife and wipe it with a vinegar-soaked cloth or kitchen paper. Cut the block of sushi into 4 lengthways, then in 4 crossways, making 16 pieces.

Arrange on a large serving plate. Put a fan-shaped piece of lemon on top. Serve with pickled ginger and a little Japanese soy sauce.

stars, hearts & flowers

Just like cookies, these children's sushi are made in pretty colours and shapes. Specially shaped moulds are sold in Japanese stores, but if you don't have access to such exciting shops, use decorative cookie cutters and other mould shapes.

½ **quantity vinegared rice (page 119)**

cherry blossom sushi

100 g/4 oz. cod or haddock fillet, skinned

2 tablespoons sugar

sea salt and pepper

red vegetable food colouring*

spring green sushi

100 g/4 oz. shelled green peas

2 teaspoons sugar

sea salt

golden star sushi

2 eggs, beaten

1 tablespoon milk

1 tablespoon sugar

star, daisy and diamond or heart shaped sushi moulds, or cookie cutters

makes 18-20

* If you don't want to use food colouring, use grilled fresh salmon, flaked, instead of the white fish and colouring.

Put the fish in a saucepan, add just enough boiling water to cover and simmer until well cooked. Drain, then carefully remove all the small bones. Pat dry with kitchen paper and put into the dry saucepan. Using a fork, crush into fine flakes. Add the sugar and a pinch of salt, then cook over a low heat, continuously stirring with a fork, for about 2 minutes, or until the fish is very dry and flaky. If using food colouring, dilute 1 drop with 1 tablespoon water, then stir quickly through the fish to spread the colour evenly. Remove from the heat and let cool. (Alternatively, use fresh salmon cooked to flakes in the same way or crush canned cooked red salmon into flakes.)

Bring a small saucepan of lightly salted water to the boil, add the peas and cook for 5 minutes or until soft. Drain and pat dry with kitchen paper. Crush with a mortar and pestle or in a food processor to form a smooth green paste. Stir in the sugar and a pinch of salt.

Lightly oil a small saucepan and heat over a moderate heat. Put the eggs, milk and sugar in a bowl, mix, then pour into the pan. Quickly stir with a fork to make soft scrambled eggs. Remove from the heat and let cool.

Divide the vinegared rice into three. To make the cherry blossom sushi, put 1 tablespoon of the pink fish flakes in the bottom of a small heart-shaped mould and press about 1 tablespoon of the rice on top. Turn out onto a plate, fish side up. Repeat until all the pink flakes and a third of the rice are used. Using a second mould, repeat using the green pea paste and another third of the rice. Using a third mould, repeat using the scrambled eggs with the remaining third of the rice. If using grilled fresh salmon, use a fourth mould.

Arrange the cherry blossom, flower, star and spring green sushi on a large plate and serve.

egg cup sushi

Hand-moulding of rice is rather a messy job and it's also difficult to make identical shapes and sizes. This simple solution uses an egg cup as a mould. These sushi are very easy to make, pretty to serve and delicious to eat.

¼ quantity vinegared rice (page 119)

5–6 smoked salmon slices, about 125 g/4½ oz., halved to make 10–12 pieces

lemon or lime wedges, to serve

a small egg cup

makes 10–12

Line an egg cup with clingfilm/plastic wrap so it hangs over the edge of the cup. Line the whole cup with a piece of smoked salmon, filling any gaps with small pieces of salmon. Put 1 tablespoon of vinegared rice in the cup and press down gently with your thumbs. Do not over-fill. Trim the excess salmon from the rim. Lift up the clingfilm/plastic wrap and turn out the moulded sushi, upside down, onto a plate. Repeat to make 10 pieces.

Arrange on a serving platter, add lemon or lime wedges and serve.

Variation Make soft scrambled eggs, using 2 eggs, 1 teaspoon sugar and a pinch of salt. Let cool. Lay a piece of clingfilm/plastic wrap in the egg cup. Put 1 teaspoon of the scrambled eggs on the bottom. Gently press to make a firm base – the egg should come about halfway up the side of the cup. Put 1 tablespoon of vinegared rice on top of the egg and again gently press down with your thumbs. Do not over-fill. Using the clingfilm/plastic wrap, turn out the moulded sushi, upside down, onto a plate. Repeat this process for the remainder of the egg and rice. Serve with a tiny bit of red caviar on top.

stuffed squid sushi

Meat is rarely used in sushi but this sweet, dry-cooked minced meat goes well with vinegared rice. It can be eaten as it is, or use it as a stuffing for squid and serve as an unusual party canapé. If you don't like to use meat, just use the squid flaps and tentacles in the sumeshi mixture, but reduce the cooking juice accordingly.

2 medium squid, cleaned

3 tablespoons sake

2–3 tablespoons Japanese rice vinegar

2 tablespoons sugar

1 tablespoon mirin (sweetened Japanese rice wine) or sweet sherry

2 tablespoons Japanese soy sauce

50 g/2 oz. minced/ground chicken or beef

2.5-cm/1-inch piece fresh ginger, peeled and finely chopped

2/3 quantity vinegared rice (page 119)

pickled ginger, to serve

makes 10–12

Peel the outer skin off the squid. It comes off easily if you hold the two flaps together and peel down the body. Put the 2 main bodies in a saucepan, add 1 tablespoon sake, cover with boiling water and simmer for 1–2 minutes. Do not overcook. Drain, rub the surface with a damp cloth to remove any marks, then sprinkle with the rice vinegar all over to retain the whiteness. Chop the flaps and tentacles.

Put the remaining sake, the sugar, mirin and soy sauce in a saucepan, mix and bring to the boil over moderate heat. Add the minced chicken or beef, the chopped squid flaps and tentacles and the chopped ginger, then stir vigorously with a fork until the meat turns white. Using a slotted spoon, transfer the cooked meat to another bowl, leaving the juice in the saucepan. Boil the juice over high heat for 1–2 minutes until thickened. Stir the meat back into the saucepan to absorb the juice and remove from the heat.

Make the vinegared rice following the method on page 119, and while still warm fold in the dry-cooked meat. Tightly stuff each squid body with half the rice mixture and, using a sharp knife, slice crossways into 5–6 pieces.

Arrange on plates and serve with pickled ginger.

hand-moulded sushi

Hand-moulded or *nigiri-zushi* is the king of all sushi. Though it looks simple, it is actually the most difficult to make and is not usually made at home, even in Japan.

⅓ **quantity vinegared rice (page 119)**

toppings

2 uncooked tiger prawn/shrimp tails

1 fillet fresh tuna or salmon, about 100 g/4 oz., skinned

1 fillet fresh white-fleshed fish such sea bream or sole, about 100 g/4 oz., skinned

100 g/4 oz. squid, cleaned and skinned

2 eggs, beaten

2 tablespoons dashi stock

1 teaspoon mirin or sweet sherry

1 teaspoon Japanese soy sauce, plus extra to serve

2 teaspoons wasabi paste or powder

2 shiso leaves or basil leaves

a small piece of nori seaweed, cut into ½-cm/¼-inch strips

sea salt

pickled ginger, to serve

cocktail sticks/toothpicks

a sushi rolling mat

makes 8–10

Skewer a cocktail stick/toothpick through each prawn/shrimp from top to tail to prevent curling while cooking. Blanch in boiling water for 2 minutes until lightly cooked and pink. Drain and put under running water. Remove and discard the cocktail sticks/toothpicks, shells and back vein. Make a slit up the belly lengthways and open out.

Slice the tuna or salmon and sea bream into rectangular pieces, 7 x 3 x 1 cm/ 3 x 1¼ x ½ inch thick. Cut the squid into similar rectangular pieces, and make fine slits on one side of each piece to make the squid more tender.

Using the beaten eggs, chicken stock, mirin and soy sauce, make an omelette following the method on page 120. Put the rolled omelette on a sushi rolling mat and tightly roll into a flat rectangular shape. When cool, cut 2 rectangular pieces, 7 x 3 x 1 cm/3 x 1¼ x ½ inch thick.

If using wasabi powder, mix with 2 teaspoons water in an egg cup and stir well to make a clay-like consistency. Leave upside down to prevent drying.

Take a handful (about 1–2 tablespoons) of the cooked rice in one hand and mould into a rectangular cylinder about 5 x 2.5 x 2.5 cm/2 x 1 x 1 inches. (Dip your fingers in hand vinegar if the rice is sticking to them.) Put a tiny bit of wasabi on top and cover with an opened prawn/shrimp.

Repeat, making 2 nigiri topped with prawns/shrimp, 2 with tuna or salmon, 2 with sea bream, 2 with squid on top of a shiso leaf and 2 with omelette. When assembling the nigiri with omelette, do not add wasabi: instead, tie with a thin nori ribbon, about ½ cm/¼ inch wide.

Arrange on a platter and serve with pickled ginger and Japanese soy sauce in a small dish. Alternatively, serve as party canapés or on small plates as part of a meal.

lettuce boats

As an alternative, serve the nigiri in lettuce 'boats'. They look very pretty and are also easier to pick up and eat – important at a party

½ quantity vinegared rice (page 119)

toppings

100 g/4 oz. beef fillet, about 7 cm/3 inches thick

vegetable oil, for rubbing

1–2 rollmops (marinated Bismarck herring)

8 asparagus tips

2 teaspoons wasabi paste or powder

4 Little Gem/romaine lettuce leaves

8 small chicory (witloof)/ Belgian endive leaves

to serve

sprigs of cress or shredded spring onions/scallions

4 small strips of nori seaweed

2.5-cm/1-inch piece fresh ginger, peeled and grated

1 spring onion/scallion, finely chopped

2 tablespoons white wine

1½ tablespoons Japanese soy sauce (shoyu)

freshly squeezed juice of ½ lemon

makes 12

Rub the beef all over with oil. Grill/broil at a high heat until golden-brown on all sides, but rare in the middle. Plunge into iced water to stop the cooking. Remove from the water, pat dry with kitchen paper and cut 4 thin slices, about 7 x 4 cm/3 x 2 inches. All the slices should be red on the inside and brown around the edges.

Cut the rollmops into 4 and make a little lengthways slit (about 3 cm/1¼ inches) in the skin of each piece.

Cook the asparagus in lightly salted water for 5 minutes until soft. Drain and place under running water to arrest cooking and bring out the colour. Pat dry with kitchen paper.

If using wasabi powder, mix with 2 teaspoons water in an egg cup, stir to make a clay-like consistency, then turn upside down to stop it drying out.

Take a handful of the cooked rice in one hand (about 1–2 tablespoons). Mould it into a rectangular shape about 5 x 2.5 x 2.5 cm/2 x 1 x 1 inches. (Dip your fingers in hand vinegar if the rice is sticking to them.) Repeat with the remaining rice, making 12 portions. Put a tiny dab of wasabi on top of 4 of the portions.

Arrange a slice of beef on 1 portion of wasabi-and-rice, with the two short sides hanging over the end. Top with a few sprigs of cress. Repeat with the other 3 slices of beef and set them in 4 Little Gem/romaine lettuce leaves.

Arrange 2 asparagus tips on another rice portion, set it in a chicory/endive leaf and tie with a nori ribbon. Repeat to make 3 more. Arrange a piece of rollmop on each of the remaining 4 rice portions and insert grated ginger and chopped spring onion/scallion into the slits.

Arrange all the leaf boats on a serving platter. Mix the white wine, soy sauce and the lemon juice in a small bowl. Serve the lettuce boats with a small bowl of lemon sauce and another of plain soy sauce.

sushi balls with roast pork & pickled plums

Pickled plums (*umeboshi*) can be bought in Japanese and Asian supermarkets. They can be very salty and sharp, so you don't need too much. If you do not like the flavour of pickled plum, replace with pickled ginger.

250 g/9 oz. pork fillet/tenderloin, in one piece

2 tablespoons Japanese soy sauce (shoyu)

1 tablespoon mirin (sweetened Japanese rice wine)

1 teaspoon Chinese hot pepper sauce or chilli sauce

½ quantity vinegared rice (page 119)

10 Japanese pickled plums, halved and pitted

makes 20

Put the pork in a plastic container. Mix the soy, mirin and hot pepper sauce in a bowl or jug/pitcher, then pour over the pork. Set aside to marinate for 1 hour, turning the pork in the marinade every 15 minutes.

Preheat the oven to 200°C (400°F) Gas 6.

Put the pork in a roasting pan and pour the marinade over the top. Roast in the preheated oven for 15 minutes. Remove from the oven, let cool, then slice thinly – you should get about 20 slices.

Divide the rice into 20 balls. Take a piece of pickled plum and push it into the centre of a rice ball, then mould the rice around it so it is completely hidden. Repeat with the remaining plums and rice. Top each ball with a slice of the marinated roast pork.

marinated beef sushi

Beef *tataki* is very rare marinated beef served in the sashimi style. If you do not like very rare beef, cook the fillet in a preheated oven at 180°C (350°F) Gas 4 for 10 minutes before returning to the pan to coat with sauce.

2 teaspoons peanut oil

300 g/10½ oz. beef eye fillet, in one piece

2 tablespoons Japanese soy sauce

2 tablespoons mirin (sweetened Japanese rice wine)

2 tablespoons rice vinegar

½ quantity vinegared rice (page 119)

shredded pickled ginger, to serve (optional)

pickled red cabbage

175 g/6 oz. (about ⅛) red cabbage

100 g/½ cup brown sugar

125 ml/½ cup red wine vinegar

makes 18

To make the pickled red cabbage, finely slice the cabbage, removing any large core pieces, and chop into 2.5-cm/1-inch lengths. Put in a medium saucepan, then add the brown sugar, vinegar and 4 tablespoons water. Bring to the boil, reduce the heat and simmer for 30 minutes.

Remove from the heat, let cool and store in a sealed container in the refrigerator for up to 1 week, or in the freezer for 3 months.

To prepare the beef, heat the oil in a frying pan and sear the beef on all sides until browned. Mix the soy sauce, mirin and vinegar in a bowl and pour over the beef, turning the beef to coat. Remove immediately from the heat and transfer the beef and its sauce to a dish. Let cool, cover and refrigerate for 1 hour, turning once.

Divide the rice into 18 balls, the size of a walnut, and shape into firm ovals.

Cut the beef in half lengthways (along the natural separation line), then slice as finely as possible. Wrap a piece of beef around the top of a rice ball and top with a little pickled cabbage or ginger.

soups & noodle bowls

Miso with ramen noodles & stir-fried vegetables
Red miso soup with tempura croutons
White miso soup with wakame, tofu & lettuce
Garlic & chilli rice soups with spring greens
Chilled somen noodles with dipping sauce
Vietnamese watercress soup
Sweet & sour tofu soup ✺ Crab noodle soup
Prawn & spinach wonton noodle soup
Prawn tom yam
Salmon, soba noodle & shiitake broth
Udon noodles with seven-spice salmon
Teriyaki mackerel & shiitake mushroom noodles
Vietnamese beef pho ✺ Vietnamese chicken pho
Vegetable & chicken ramen
Thai chicken, mushroom & coconut soup
Spring chicken soup with rice noodles & herbs
Duck soup ✺ Thai pork & rice soup
Sparerib & tamarind soup

miso with ramen noodles & stir-fried vegetables

Japanese broths are hearty and comforting and often packed with fresh and earthy cold-weather vegetables. The broths themselves are generally made with a base of simple stock and soy sauce or miso. This prepared, soya bean paste is probably the most essential Japanese food item with a very strong 'umami' (savoury) flavour component and is easily found in the Asian foods aisle at your supermarket or a speciality food store. The noodles, although common in Japan, are Chinese wheat-based noodles and, when bought dried, are a very handy staple

3 tablespoons red miso paste

1 tablespoon light soy sauce

½ teaspoon white sugar

1.25 litres/5 cups vegetable stock

200 g/7 oz. ramen or thin egg noodles

1 tablespoon light olive oil

2 teaspoons sesame oil

2 teaspoons finely sliced fresh ginger

2 shallots, thinly sliced

2 leeks, julienned

200 g/7 oz. Savoy cabbage leaves, finely shredded

200 g/7 oz. red cabbage, finely shredded

serves 4

Combine the miso, soy sauce, sugar and stock in a large saucepan set over medium heat and warm until the miso has completely dissolved. Keep warm over low heat. Cook the noodles according to the packet instructions. Drain well and divide between 4 warmed serving bowls.

Put the oils in a wok or large frying pan set over high heat. Add the ginger and shallots and cook for just a few seconds to flavour the oil. Add the leeks and cabbage and stir-fry for 2 minutes, until the vegetables are crisp and glistening with oil.

Ladle the warm miso mixture over the noodles and top with the stir-fried vegetables. Serve immediately.

red miso soup with tempura croutons

You need only about one-third of this batter for this recipe, but half an egg seems difficult to work with, so use the rest of the batter for tempura vegetables or prawns/shrimp. Alternatively, you could use the pressed croutons sold in Japanese stores.

1 litre/4 cups dashi stock

3 tablespoons red miso paste

2 spring onions/scallions, finely sliced

tempura croutons

1 egg, separated

1 tablespoon freshly squeezed lemon juice

150 ml/²/₃ cup iced water

60 g/½ cup plain/all-purpose flour

peanut or safflower oil, for frying

serves 4

To make the batter, put the egg yolk, lemon juice and iced water in a bowl. Whisk gently, then whisk in the flour to form a smooth batter. Do not overmix.

Whisk the egg white in a second bowl until stiff but not dry, then fold into the batter.

To cook the croutons, fill a large wok or saucepan one-third full with oil and heat to 190°C (375°F), or until a small cube of bread cooked in the oil turns golden in 30 seconds.

Carefully drop teaspoons of the batter into the oil and cook for 30 seconds until crispy. Scoop out and drain on kitchen paper.

Pour the dashi into a saucepan, bring to the boil, then reduce to a simmer. Mix the miso paste with a few tablespoons of the dashi to loosen it, then stir it into the simmering stock. Divide the stock between 4 bowls, add the croutons and spring onions/scallions and serve.

white miso soup with wakame, tofu & lettuce

The more mellow flavours of white miso make a perfect drink to serve with sushi rolls – the delicious and delicate taste of this soup will not overpower even the most subtle of sushi.

a pinch of wakame (dried seaweed)

1 litre/4 cups dashi stock

4 tablespoons white miso paste

100 g/4 oz. silken tofu, cut into ¹/₂-cm/¹/₄-inch cubes

¹/₄ iceberg or other crisp lettuce, finely sliced (optional)

serves 4

Soak the wakame in a bowl of hot water for 15 minutes, then drain.

Pour the dashi stock into a saucepan, bring to the boil, then reduce to a simmer. Mix the miso paste in a bowl with a few tablespoons of the dashi to loosen it, then stir it into the simmering stock. Add the tofu and wakame and cook in the soup for 1 minute.

Divide the lettuce, if using, between 4 bowls, ladle the hot soup over the top, then serve.

garlic & chilli rice soup with spring greens

This is a substantial soup – really more of a light stew. Boiled rice soups are popular in many Asian countries, especially China where they are called *congees*. They are often eaten for breakfast, but are an acquired taste as the rice is boiled until it breaks down to form a rather viscous white 'porridge'. The greens can be spring greens/collards or the fresh, young outer leaves of brassicas such as cabbage. They work very nicely with the simple Asian flavours here.

1 tablespoon vegetable oil

2 teaspoons sesame oil

2 garlic cloves, chopped

4 spring onions/scallions, finely chopped

2 teaspoons finely grated fresh ginger

1 small red chilli, deseeded and thinly sliced

100 g/½ cup long-grain white rice

1.5 litres/6 cups vegetable stock

1 tablespoon soy sauce or Thai fish sauce

1 bunch of spring greens/collard greens, roughly shredded

1 small bunch of fresh coriander/cilantro, chopped

white pepper

serves 2

Put the oils in a saucepan and set over high heat. Add the garlic and spring onions/scallions and cook until the garlic is turning golden and just starting to burn. This will give the soup a lovely, nutty garlic flavour. Add the ginger, chilli and rice to the pan and stir-fry in the garlic-infused oil for 1 minute. Add the stock and soy sauce and bring to the boil.

Cover with a lid and cook over low heat for 30 minutes, until the rice is soft and the soup has thickened. Add the spring/collard greens and cook for 5 minutes, until they turn emerald green and are tender. Ladle the soup into warmed serving bowls, sprinkle the coriander/cilantro over the top and season to taste with pepper.

chilled somen noodles with dipping sauce

As the weather in Japan can get very hot, chilled noodles are a popular summer dish. Somen are very fine wheat noodles, and are easy to find in larger supermarkets or Asian grocers. Also available in Asian stores is instant dashi (used here to flavour the soy dipping sauce), a basic stock that is a key ingredient in Japanese cuisine.

about 400 g/14 oz. dried somen noodles (75 g/3 oz. per person as a starter, 100 g/4 oz. as a main/entrée)

soy dipping sauce

8 dried shiitake mushrooms

250 ml/1 cup dashi stock

125 ml/½ cup mirin (sweetened Japanese rice wine) or dry sherry

60 ml/¼ cup soy sauce

to serve

2.5-cm/1-inch piece fresh ginger, peeled and finely grated

1 sheet dried nori seaweed, thinly sliced

8 spring onions/scallions, finely chopped diagonally

1 baby cucumber, peeled and thinly sliced

8 cooked prawns/shrimp, peeled, but with tail fins intact

serves 4–6

Put the shiitake mushrooms into a bowl and cover with hot water. Leave to rehydrate for at least 15 minutes or until softened. Drain, reserving the soaking liquid. Cut off and discard the hard stems and thinly slice the caps.

Put the dashi into a saucepan and heat gently until almost boiling. Reduce the heat immediately, add the mirin and soy sauce and return to the boil. Turn off the heat and let cool to room temperature. You may prepare up to this point the day before and refrigerate until ready to use.

Bring a large saucepan of water to the boil and add the noodles, one bundle at a time. Stir with chopsticks each time you add a bundle to make sure they separate. Watch the saucepan carefully and stand by with a glass of cold water ready.

When the water begins to boil over, add the cold water. This is called *bikkuri mizu* ('surprise water') and it is used to make the outside and inside of the noodles cook at the same speed. Return to the boil and turn off the heat. Drain and rinse the noodles under cold running water, drain again and chill.

To serve, float the noodles in a large glass bowl or separate small bowls, filled with ice and water. Put the ginger, seaweed, spring onions/scallions, cucumber and prawns/shrimp on a separate plate and put the soy dipping sauce in a bowl. Guests can choose their own combinations.

Vietnamese watercress soup

In Vietnam, this traditional soup is made with chrysanthemum leaves, and if you have access to a good Asian greengrocer, you can try it made in the classic way. Watercress however, with its peppery flavour and the texture-contrast between soft leaves and crunchy stems, is a good substitute. Add it at the very end, because it wilts very fast. If fish sauce is hard to find, use extra salt instead.

2 tablespoons peanut oil

12 uncooked prawns/shrimp, peeled but with shells reserved*

2.5-cm/1-inch piece fresh ginger, sliced and crushed

1 lemongrass stalk, halved lengthways and crushed lightly

3 garlic cloves, finely sliced

1 litre/4 cups boiling fish stock

8 spring onions/scallions, white and green, halved crossways and bruised

2 tablespoons fish sauce, such as Vietnamese nuoc mam or Thai nam pla

1 tablespoon sugar

1 teaspoon sea salt

1 large bunch watercress, washed well, dried and trimmed

serves 4

*Note: The prawn/shrimp shells are included in this recipe because they give terrific flavour. If yours are already shelled, omit this step and stir-fry the ginger, garlic and lemongrass at the same time as the prawns/shrimp, but remove the lemongrass and ginger before serving. For a more substantial soup, add your choice of soaked or fresh noodles with the stock.

Heat the oil in a wok, add the prawn/shrimp shells, ginger, lemongrass and garlic and stir-fry until the shells change colour. Keep stir-frying for a few minutes to extract some of the flavour and colour and then transfer to the pan of fish stock.

Add the spring onions/scallions to the wok and stir-fry for 2 minutes. Add the shelled prawns/shrimp and stir-fry until they become opaque. Add the fish sauce, sugar and salt, strain in the fish stock and return to the boil.

Divide the spring onions/scallions and prawns/shrimp between 4 deep soup bowls, then ladle in the stock. Add large handfuls of watercress and serve.

sweet & sour tofu soup

Thai food has become popular because it offers such a variety of tastes, flavours and textures – many of which are combined in this delicious soup. Red vinegar is widely available in Asian supermarkets, but if you can't find it you can use white instead.

1.25 litres/5 cups vegetable stock

1 tablespoon cornflour/cornstarch

60 g/2½ oz. pickled cabbage, chopped into 2.5-cm/1-inch lengths

60 g/2½ oz. bamboo shoots, cut into matchsticks

4–5 ears of baby corn, chopped into rings

60 g/½ cup shelled peas, fresh or frozen

125 g/4½ oz. soft white tofu, cut into ½-cm/¼-inch cubes

60 g/2½ oz. lump crabmeat

½ small red or green bell pepper, finely chopped

2 tablespoons light soy sauce

2 tablespoons Thai fish sauce

1 tablespoon vinegar, preferably red vinegar

1 teaspoon sugar

½ teaspoon freshly ground white pepper

fresh coriander/cilantro leaves, to serve

serves 4

Put the stock in a large saucepan and bring to the boil. Put the cornflour/cornstarch in a cup, stir in about 1 tablespoon water, then stir the mixture into the stock to thicken it slightly.

Add the cabbage, bamboo shoots and corn, then stir in the peas, tofu, crabmeat, sweet pepper, soy sauce, fish sauce, red vinegar, sugar and pepper, stirring constantly.

Ladle at once into a serving bowl and top with coriander/cilantro leaves.

Crab noodle soup

This aromatic noodle soup is a speciality of central Vietnam, where all productive land is given over to cultivating rice. The authentic recipe uses tiny freshwater crabs commonly found in paddy fields. Usually they are pounded almost to a paste and made into small dumplings, but this recipe is easier with the crabmeat floating freely in the soup.

400 g/14 oz. dried rice vermicelli noodles

4 tablespoons Asian dried shrimp

2 tablespoons peanut oil

4 shallots, thinly sliced

2 garlic cloves, crushed

2 red chillies, deseeded and finely chopped

4 tomatoes, deseeded and coarsely chopped

200 g/7 oz. cooked white crabmeat, flaked

1.25 litres/5 cups chicken stock

2 tablespoons Asian fish sauce

1 teaspoon soft light brown sugar

1 tablespoon rice vinegar

½ iceberg lettuce, finely sliced

to serve

2 spring onions/scallions, finely chopped

a handful of fresh mint leaves

a handful of fresh coriander/ cilantro leaves

1 lime, cut into 4 wedges

serves 4

Put the noodles into a bowl and cover with boiling water for 10 minutes, or until soft. Drain, rinse under cold running water and drain again. Using kitchen scissors, chop them into manageable lengths, about 5 cm/2 inches, and set aside.

Put the dried shrimp into another bowl, add 125 ml/½ cup boiling water and soak for 20 minutes. Drain and reserve the shrimp and their soaking water.

Heat the oil in a wok, swirl to coat, then add the shallots, garlic and chillies. Stir-fry for 1 minute, then add the tomatoes, crabmeat, soaked shrimp, their soaking water and the chicken stock. Season the soup with fish sauce, sugar and vinegar and bring to the boil. Reduce the heat to low and let simmer for 5 minutes.

Turn off the heat and stir in the noodles and lettuce.

Ladle the soup into 4 bowls and serve with the spring onions/scallions, mint and coriander/cilantro leaves and lime wedges on top.

prawn & spinach wonton noodle soup

This is the Cantonese equivalent of Italian ravioli, though the Chinese would claim that theirs came first. The wonton wrapper is made from egg noodle dough and can be bought fresh or frozen from Asian grocers. The size of wrappers and packets varies, but this recipe uses twenty of the 7-cm/3-inch size. Any leftover wrappers can be frozen.

200 g/8 oz. fresh or dried egg noodles

1 litre/4 cups chicken stock

1 tablespoon soy sauce

100 g/4 oz. Chinese greens such as Chinese/Napa cabbage or bok choy, coarsely chopped

sea salt and freshly ground black pepper

2 spring onions/scallions, sliced diagonally, to serve

wontons

2 tablespoons peanut oil

50 g/2 oz. spinach, coarsely chopped

100 g/4 oz. uncooked prawns/shrimp, peeled, deveined and finely chopped

1 garlic clove, crushed

2.5-cm/1-inch piece fresh ginger, peeled and finely chopped

150 g/5 oz. minced/ground pork

1 egg, separated

20 fresh wonton wrappers

sea salt and freshly ground black pepper

serves 4

To make the wontons, heat the oil in a wok. Add the spinach and stir-fry over medium heat until soft. Remove from the heat, let cool a little, then squeeze out as much excess juice as possible.

Transfer the spinach to a large bowl, add the prawns/shrimp, garlic, ginger, pork, egg yolk, salt and pepper and mix well.

Put a heaped teaspoon of the pork mixture in the centre of a wonton wrapper. Brush the edges of the wrapper with lightly beaten egg white and fold in half to make a triangle.

Wet the two bottom corners of the triangle and seal them together. (You can prepare up to this point 6 hours in advance and keep the wontons covered and refrigerated.)

Bring a large saucepan of water to the boil, add the fresh noodles, if using, and cook for 2-3 minutes. (If you are using dry noodles, cook for about 3-5 minutes.) Scoop out the cooked noodles with a strainer and divide between 4 serving bowls - keep the water simmering.

Put the chicken stock into a second saucepan and heat to simmering - try not to boil or the stock will be cloudy. Season with soy sauce, salt and pepper and keep it simmering.

Return the water to the boil and cook the wontons in batches of 4-5 for 5 minutes each.

Spoon them out and add them to the serving bowls. Using the same boiling water, blanch the Chinese greens for 1 minute, then immediately remove and add to the serving bowls. Ladle the stock into the bowls, top with the spring onions/scallions and serve immediately.

prawn tom yam

This soup is so satisfying and just goes to show that flavour doesn't need to come from butter or cream. The end result is based on a good backbone of flavour which comes from a rich chicken stock. All the other aromatics need to be balanced against each other, so taste before serving and make any necessary adjustments.

1 litre/4 cups chicken stock

1 lemongrass stalk, halved lengthways and bruised

2.5-cm/1-inch piece fresh ginger, peeled and thinly sliced

3 kaffir lime leaves

a small handful of fresh coriander/cilantro, stalks finely chopped and leaves left whole

2 shallots, sliced

3 chillies, deseeded and shredded

150 g/5 oz. button mushrooms, halved

200 g/7 oz. uncooked king prawns/shrimp, deveined and shelled but tails left intact

80 ml/⅓ cup freshly squeezed lime juice

2 tablespoons sugar

4 tablespoons fish sauce

serves 4–6

Put the chicken stock in a large saucepan with the lemongrass, ginger, lime leaves, chopped coriander/cilantro stalks, shallots, chillies and mushrooms. Bring to the boil, turn down the heat and simmer for 10 minutes.

Butterfly the prawns/shrimp (cut down the back lengthways with a sharp knife) and add them to the pan with the lime juice, sugar and fish sauce and simmer for 1 minute or until the prawns/shrimp are pink. Scatter the coriander/cilantro leaves into the soup. Take off the heat and taste, adding more fish sauce, lime juice or sugar, as you see fit.

Divide the soup between 4-6 bowls and serve.

salmon, soba noodle & shiitake broth

Shiitake mushrooms have a unique, earthy savouriness that few other non-meaty ingredients have and which the Japanese call 'umami'. This means they can make a light broth very flavoursome. Soba noodles are made from buckwheat and go well with the delicate salmon.

1 tablespoon groundnut oil

250 g/9 oz. shiitake mushrooms, washed, dried and halved

2.5-cm/1-inch piece fresh ginger, unpeeled and sliced

three 8-g/¼-oz. sachets miso stock powder

1.5 litres/6 cups boiling water

200 g/7 oz. buckwheat soba noodles

2 tablespoons light soy sauce

4 tablespoons sake

2 tablespoons granulated sugar

four 125-g/4½-oz. salmon fillets, cut into chunks

6 spring onions/scallions, sliced

a pinch of chilli powder

sesame oil, to drizzle

serves 4

Heat the oil in a large saucepan over medium heat and add the mushrooms and ginger. Cook gently for 5 minutes, or until softened.

Put the miso stock powder and boiling water in a jug/pitcher and stir until dissolved. Pour into the pan with the mushrooms. Bring to the boil and simmer for 5 minutes to allow the flavours to infuse. Add the noodles and bring to the boil, then cook for a further 4 minutes, or until just tender (they will continue to cook while you dish up so don't overdo them). Add the soy sauce, sake and sugar to the broth and gently lower in the salmon. Reduce the heat to low so the broth is only just boiling and poach the salmon for 3–4 minutes, or until cooked through.

Fish out the noodles and transfer to bowls. Using a slotted spoon, lift out the salmon and place on top of the noodles. Ladle the remaining soup into the bowls, scatter with the spring onions/scallions and chilli powder and drizzle with sesame oil. Serve immediately.

udon noodles with seven-spice salmon

The instant dashi stock and miso soup stock used in Japanese cooking are available from some larger supermarkets or Asian food stores, along with the seven-spice pepper. Alternatively use good-quality fresh fish stock.

250 g/9 oz. udon noodles

1.5 litres/6 cups dashi or miso stock (see recipe introduction)

50 ml/¼ cup mirin (sweetened Japanese rice wine)

50 ml/¼ cup dark soy sauce

100 g/4 oz. firm tofu, cubed

6 spring onions/scallions, trimmed and sliced

a few strands of dried wakame seaweed

4 salmon fillets, 200 g/8 oz. each

1 tablespoon sunflower or peanut oil

Japanese seven-spice pepper (*shichimi togarashi*)

serves 4

To cook the noodles, plunge them into a saucepan of boiling water, return to the boil and simmer for 4 minutes until tender. Drain and refresh under cold water, drain again and pat dry with kitchen paper.

Put the dashi or miso stock into a saucepan, add the mirin, soy sauce, tofu, spring onions/scallions and wakame and bring to the boil.

Brush the salmon with the oil and dust with a little seven-spice powder (go easy with the pepper – it is quite hot!). Put the fillets skin side down on a preheated stove-top grill pan for 4 minutes, then turn and cook for a further 1 minute.

Divide the noodles between 4 deep warmed soup bowls, then add the stock, tofu and vegetables. Put the salmon on top and serve.

teriyaki mackerel & shiitake noodle soup

Japanese broths always feel like they are doing you the world of good. Shiitake mushrooms have that unique savoury 'umami' flavour to them that feels really satisfying. If you can't get hold of kombu (a Japanese seaweed sold dried in packets) and bonito flakes, you could use a fish stock mixed with miso soup.

200 g/7 oz. shiitake mushrooms, sliced

200 g/7 oz. udon noodles

100 g/4 oz. baby spinach leaves

1 tablespoon light soy sauce

6 spring onions/scallions, shredded and left in iced water to curl

teriyaki mackerel

3 tablespoons light soy sauce

2 tablespoons sake

2 teaspoons sugar

½ teaspoon freshly grated ginger

4 mackerel fillets

ginger dashi

15-cm/6-inch piece kombu or 1 tablespoon instant dashi with bonito flakes

5-cm/2-inch piece fresh ginger, peeled and thinly sliced

serves 4

To make the teriyaki, mix the soy sauce, sake, sugar and ginger together in a shallow dish. Add the fish, toss well to coat in the teriyaki and marinate for 15 minutes while you make the dashi.

To make the dashi, put the kombu and 1 litre/4 cups water in a saucepan and gently heat, skimming off any scum. Just before it boils, remove and discard the kombu. Add the ginger to the water, bring to the boil, then strain though a fine sieve into a large saucepan. Alternatively, make up 800 ml/3¼ cups instant dashi in a large saucepan. Add the shiitake mushrooms to the homemade or instant dashi and cook for 5 minutes or until softening.

Preheat the grill/broiler.

Cook the noodles in a large pan of water according to the packet instructions, drain and run under cold water. Put the marinated fish on a baking sheet and grill/broil for 3 minutes on each side until cooked through. Add the spinach to the dashi, along with the noodles.

Divide the soup between 4 bowls, season with soy sauce, top with a piece of fish and scatter with the spring onions/scallions.

Vietnamese beef pho

This is Vietnamese fast food – it's slurped down in a flash but be warned that it takes time to make. It's pronounced 'fuh' and derives from the French *pot au feu* ('pot on fire'). It's a soothing, deeply flavoured broth bobbing with slices of beef, rice noodles and perky beansprouts and served with a bowl of Thai basil, mint, chilli and lime which you add to your own taste.

1 tablespoon sunflower oil

1 star anise

2 lemongrass stalks, sliced

1 cinnamon stick

1 tablespoon coriander seeds

1 tablespoon black peppercorns

3-cm/1¼-inch piece fresh ginger, sliced

4 garlic cloves, peeled and bruised

1.5 litres/6 cups beef stock

3 fresh coriander/cilantro sprigs, roots included

150 g/5 oz. rice noodles

4 tablespoons freshly squeezed lime juice

2 tablespoons fish sauce

200 g/7 oz. sirloin steak, thinly sliced

100 g/1 cup beansprouts

3 shallots, thinly sliced

to serve

a handful of fresh Thai basil leaves

several fresh mint leaves

1 red chilli, sliced

lime wedges

serves 4

Heat the sunflower oil in a large saucepan over low heat, then add the anise, lemongrass, cinnamon, coriander seeds, peppercorns, ginger and garlic. Cook gently for 1–2 minutes to release their aromas. Pour in the stock and bring to the boil.

Add the coriander/cilantro sprigs and simmer for 30 minutes. Take off the heat and leave to infuse while you prepare the other ingredients.

Get ready a plate of condiments. Pile up the Thai basil, mint, chilli and lime wedges on a plate and keep in the fridge until you're ready.

When you're ready to eat, cook the rice noodles in a large pan of boiling water according to the packet instructions. Drain and refresh under cold running water. Divide between 4 bowls.

Strain the stock back into the pan and add enough lime juice and fish sauce to taste. Add the beef and cook for 1 minute, or until it is just cooked through. Ladle the beef and stock onto the noodles and scatter the beansprouts and shallots over the top. Serve with the plate of condiments so everyone can season to taste.

Vietnamese chicken pho

This is a chicken version of the classic Vietnamese beef pho. It is every bit as full of complex flavours, but lighter and perhaps more subtle than the beef version. It is very important to use a good quality chicken as this determines the flavour of the soup.

2 teaspoons brown sugar

4 tablespoons fish sauce

250 g/9 oz. fresh rice noodles

sea salt and freshly ground black pepper

4 tablespoons crisp deep-fried shallots, to serve

Asian chicken stock

1 whole small free-range chicken, about 1.5 kg/3 lbs.

1 tablespoon salt

2 red onions, halved

1 cinnamon stick

2.5-cm/1-inch piece fresh ginger, thickly sliced

1 whole star anise

4 cardamom pods, crushed

2 kaffir lime leaves, roughly torn

table salad

200 g/2 cups fresh beansprouts, rinsed, drained and trimmed

a handful of fresh mint

a handful of fresh Thai basil

a handful of fresh coriander/cilantro leaves

2 spring onions/scallions, chopped

2 fresh red chillies, finely chopped

1 lime, cut into 4 wedges

To make the stock, put the chicken into a large saucepan, then add the salt, onions, cinnamon stick, ginger, star anise, cardamom pods and lime leaves. Add 3 litres/3 quarts water and bring to the boil over medium heat and skim off the foam. Reduce the heat to low and let simmer for 3–6 hours. Remove the chicken from the pan and strain the stock through a fine sieve into a bowl. Reserve the chicken, keeping it warm in a low oven.*

Ladle 1 litre/4 cups of the stock into a saucepan and season with sugar and fish sauce. Taste and adjust the seasoning with salt and pepper.

Put the rice noodles into a bowl, cover with boiling water and stir gently with chopsticks to separate. Drain immediately and pour into 4 large soup bowls.

Shred the meat from the chicken thighs and breasts with a fork. Put the shredded chicken on top of the noodles and ladle in the hot soup. Sprinkle with deep-fried shallots.

Serve with a plate of table salad – beansprouts, herbs, spring onions/scallions, chillies and lime wedges for each person to add according to taste.

*Note If the stock is being prepared for use in the Duck Soup on page 95, the chicken can be reserved for use in another dish – it is delicious shredded into salads or soups.

serves 4

vegetable & chicken ramen

Don't be put off by the long list of ingredients here – this Japanese-style soup couldn't be easier to make, and is light, soothing and nourishing. It is perfect for a quick and healthy mid-week supper.

2 skinless, boneless chicken breasts, about 150 g/5½ oz. each, sliced into thin strips

100 g/4 oz. soba noodles

750 ml/3 cups hot water

2 tablespoons brown rice miso paste

1 tablespoon soy sauce

2.5-cm/1-inch piece fresh ginger, peeled and cut into thin strips

1 carrot, peeled, halved and cut into thin strips

3 spring onions/scallions, diagonally sliced

½ red bell pepper, deseeded and cut into thin strips

2 pak-choi, halved lengthways

½ teaspoon toasted sesame oil

a sprinkling of toasted nori (seaweed) flakes

2 tablespoons chopped fresh coriander/cilantro leaves

sunflower or rapeseed/canola oil, for brushing

serves 2

Preheat the grill/broiler to high and line the grill/broiler pan with foil.

Arrange the chicken in the grill/broiler pan and brush with oil. Grill/broil for 5–6 minutes each side until cooked through and there is no trace of pink in the centre.

Meanwhile, cook the soba noodles in plenty of boiling water following the instructions on the packet, then drain and refresh under cold running water. Set aside.

Put the hot water in a saucepan, add the miso paste and stir until dissolved. Add the soy sauce, ginger, carrot, spring onions/scallions, red pepper and pak-choi and bring up to boiling point. Reduce the heat and simmer for about 3 minutes until the pak-choi is just tender. Stir in the sesame oil.

Divide the noodles between 2 shallow bowls and spoon over the vegetables and stock. Slice the chicken breasts and place on top, sprinkle with the nori and coriander/cilantro leaves, then serve.

thai chicken, mushroom & coconut soup

This is a classic Thai soup called *Tom Ka Gai*. It shouldn't sting the senses with chilli, which is how some restaurants make it; it should soothe and warm and feel as though it is replenishing your energy. You can serve it without the rice noodles as a first course.

125 g/4½ oz. rice noodles

400 ml/1⅔ cups coconut milk

200 ml/¾ cup chicken stock

2 lemongrass stalks, halved lengthways and bruised

5-cm/2-inch piece fresh galangal or ginger, peeled and sliced

5 kaffir lime leaves

3 tablespoons demerara sugar

2 tablespoons fish sauce

3 red bird's-eye chillies, bruised

200 g/7 oz. chicken breast or thigh, skinless and sliced into 2.5-cm/1-inch strips

150 g/5 oz. oyster mushrooms, halved

freshly squeezed juice of 1–2 limes

fresh coriander/cilantro leaves, to serve

serves 4

Put the noodles in a bowl and cover with boiling water. Leave to soak for 20 minutes while you make the rest of the soup.

Put the coconut milk, stock, lemongrass, galangal and lime leaves in a large saucepan and slowly bring to the boil over medium heat. Add the sugar, fish sauce, chillies, chicken and mushrooms and simmer for 6–8 minutes until the chicken is cooked through. Stir in the lime juice and taste. If it needs more salt, add a dash of fish sauce and if it is hot and salty, it may need rounding off with a touch more sugar.

Drain the noodles and divide between 4 bowls. Ladle the soup over the noodles, garnish with the coriander/cilantro and serve.

spring chicken soup with rice noodles & herbs

All you need for this light refreshing soup is a lovely young, organic chicken, some fresh spring herbs and a visit to your local speciality Asian store. Dead simple and so full of the fresh flavours of spring. For authenticity, use Thai basil if you can find it, but don't worry if you cannot, it's the aniseed flavour of basil you need here so any variety will do.

1 small free-range spring chicken, weighing about 1 kg/2¼ lbs.

2 star anise

1 cinnamon stick

2 tablespoons Thai fish sauce, plus extra for seasoning

200 g/7 oz. rice stick noodles, about 1 cm/½ inch wide

a large handful of fresh mint leaves

a handful of fresh basil (ideally Thai) leaves, torn

a large handful of fresh coriander/ cilantro leaves

180 g/1½ cups beansprouts

2 limes, cut into wedges

serves 4

Wash the chicken well. Put the chicken in a large saucepan and cover with 3 litres/3 quarts cold water. Add the star anise and cinnamon to the pan and put over high heat. Bring the water to the boil, reduce the heat to low and simmer for 15 minutes. Cover the pan with a tight-fitting lid, remove from the heat and let the chicken poach for 1 hour. Remove the chicken from the pan and pour 2 litres/2 quarts of the stock into a clean saucepan (keep the remaining stock for later use). Add the fish sauce to the stock and simmer over low heat. When the chicken is cool enough to handle shred the meat, discarding the skin and bones.

Put the noodles in a heatproof bowl, cover with boiling water and let stand for 10 minutes, or until soft. Drain well and divide between 4 serving bowls. Top with the chicken and ladle over the hot broth. Top each soup with some herbs and beansprouts and serve with fresh lime wedges on the side to squeeze over and some fish sauce to season.

Variation The flesh of poached chicken is soft and succulent which makes it perfect for throwing in a salad or a light Thai or Indian curry.

duck soup

You can buy Thai curry pastes almost everywhere these days, but they're not hard to make yourself. If you would prefer to buy it, go to an Asian market where it will be closer to the real thing. These markets will also sell the yellow, egg-shaped aubergines.

4 tablespoons peanut oil

1–2 skinless duck breasts

150 g/5 oz. dried wide rice stick noodles (optional)

3 egg-shaped yellow, white or purple aubergines/eggplants, or small Chinese aubergines/eggplants, quartered and deseeded (optional)

1 teaspoon sugar

2 tablespoons fish sauce, or to taste

1 litre/4 cups Asian Chicken Stock (page 87)

6 Chinese yard-long beans, sliced into 2.5-cm/1-inch pieces, or 250 g/9 oz. green beans

Thai red curry paste

5–10 dried red chillies, soaked in hot water for 30 minutes, then drained

1/2 teaspoon coriander seeds

1/2 teaspoon cumin seeds

1 garlic clove, crushed

2–3 small shallots

2.5-cm/1-inch piece fresh ginger or galangal, finely sliced

freshly grated zest of 1 lime, preferably a kaffir lime

1 tablespoon fish sauce

2–3 limes, cut into wedges, to serve

chopped chillies, to serve

To make the curry paste, remove the seeds from the chillies if you like. Stir-fry the coriander and cumin seeds in a dry frying pan for 2 minutes to release the aromas. Let cool. Put all the paste ingredients in a spice grinder or blender and purée in bursts. Use 2–4 tablespoons for this recipe and freeze the remainder.

To prepare the duck breasts, preheat a wok, add 2 tablespoons of the peanut oil and sear the duck breasts on all sides. You are just sealing the outside – the inside should be raw. Remove, cool and freeze. Just before cooking, slice them very finely.

Soak the noodles, if using, in hot water for 15 minutes. Boil for 1–2 minutes, then drain and plunge into cold water.

Add the remaining 2 tablespoons peanut oil to the wok, add the aubergine/eggplant pieces, if using, and stir-fry until browned on the edges and softened. Remove and set aside.

Add the 2–4 tablespoons curry paste to the wok and stir-fry gently to release the aromas. Add the sugar and stir-fry for a minute or so. Add 1 tablespoon of the fish sauce and stir-fry again. Add the stock and bring to the boil. Add the aubergines/eggplant, if using, and the beans. Return to the boil and simmer for 15 minutes. Taste, add extra fish sauce as needed, and set aside for 15 minutes.

When ready to serve, reheat the vegetables and stock, drain the noodles, cover with boiling water, then drain again.

Divide the noodles and vegetables between large bowls. Add the duck, ladle in boiling stock (which instantly cooks the duck), and serve with extra lime wedges and a dish of chopped chillies.

serves 4

Thai pork & rice soup

These brothy soups have a purity to them; it makes them simple and complex at the same time. You can ring the changes with this combination and make the meatballs into wontons if you happen to have some wonton wrappers from the Asian grocers. Simply envelope the meatballs in a triangle and then pinch the ends of the wonton wrapper together. Or you could add a handful of slippery noodles instead of the rice.

meatballs

3 garlic cloves, chopped

**a small handful of fresh coriander/
cilantro, leaves and roots**

450 g/1 lb. minced/ground pork

2 teaspoons fish sauce

¼ teaspoon white pepper

soup

1.25 litres/5 cups chicken stock

**2.5-cm/1-inch piece fresh ginger,
peeled and shredded**

1 teaspoon sugar

1 tablespoon fish sauce

100 g/1 cup shredded Chinese cabbage

**100 g/1 cup cooked short grain rice
or 150 g/5 oz. rice stick noodles**

to serve

6 spring onions/scallions, shredded

1 teaspoon sesame oil, to drizzle

serves 4

To make the meatballs, put the garlic and coriander/cilantro in a food processor and blend together until chopped. Add the pork, fish sauce and pepper and process. Wet your hands and roll the mixture into 2.5-cm/1-inch meatballs. Chill in the refrigerator until needed.

To make the soup, heat the stock with the ginger, sugar and fish sauce and leave it to bubble for 5 minutes. Lower in the pork meatballs and gently simmer for 3 minutes (the water should be barely bubbling). Add the cabbage and rice and simmer for a further 2 minutes, or until the meatballs are cooked through.

Divide the soup between 4 bowls, scatter with spring onions/scallions and drizzle with sesame oil.

sparerib & tamarind soup

While *Tom Yam* is well known in Western countries, *Tom Som* is less so, although it is an equal favourite inside Thailand. However, that lack of familiarity in the West can change because the ingredients are now more widely available. The sparerib-based stock includes a mixture of garlic, shallots, ginger and tamarind water – the latter contributing its strong, sour taste. It offers an exciting alternative to the traditional Tom Yam soup.

1 teaspoon black peppercorns

1 tablespoon finely chopped fresh coriander/cilantro root

2 garlic cloves

4 small shallots

1 tablespoon peanut or sunflower oil

1.25 litres/5 cups chicken stock

500 g/1 lb. small pork spareribs, chopped into 2.5-cm/ 1-inch pieces

5-cm/2-inch piece fresh ginger, finely sliced into matchsticks

2 tablespoons tamarind water

2 tablespoons sugar

3 tablespoons Thai fish sauce

4 spring onions/scallions, chopped into 2.5-cm/ 1-inch lengths

serves 4

Using a mortar and pestle, pound the peppercorns, coriander/cilantro root, garlic and shallots to form a paste.

Heat the oil in a large saucepan, add the paste and fry for 5 seconds, stirring well. Add the stock and bring to the boil, stirring well. Add the spareribs and return to the boil.

Add the ginger, tamarind water, sugar, fish sauce and spring onions/scallions. Return to the boil again and simmer for 1 minute. Ladle into bowls and serve.

Note Preparing tamarind

If you can't find tamarind water, or the pulp in block form, tamarind paste is available in small bottles in Asian supermarkets. For this recipe, mix 1 tablespoon paste with 1 tablespoon water.

Tamarind pulp is also available in block form. To prepare your own tamarind water, mix 1 tablespoon tamarind pulp in a bowl with 150 ml/⅔ cup hot water, mashing with a fork. As you mix the pulp and water, the water absorbs the taste of the tamarind. When the water is cool, you can squeeze the tamarind pulp to extract more juice (and you can remove any seeds). Pour off the juice into a container and set aside for use in recipes. It will keep for about a week in the refrigerator.

salads

Warm tossed Asian coleslaw
Pickled spring vegetable & marinated tofu salad
Japanese garden salad with noodles
Vermicelli salad
Lobster noodle salad with coconut & fruit
Sesame chicken & vegetable noodle salad
Ginger duck salad

warm tossed Asian coleslaw

Classic coleslaw is revamped here by replacing the mayonnaise with a Vietnamese-inspired peanut and lime dressing and by enhancing the shredded cabbage and carrot mix with crunchy beansprouts and coriander/cilantro leaves. Remember not to toss the vegetables in the warm sauce until just before serving so that they don't lose their crunch.

1 tablespoon peanut oil

1 shallot, finely chopped

2 garlic cloves, finely chopped

1 large red chilli, deseeded and thinly sliced

150 g/1½ cups very thinly sliced white cabbage

150 g/1½ cups very thinly sliced red cabbage

1 large carrot, cut into very thin matchsticks

100 g/1 cup beansprouts

a small bunch of fresh coriander/ cilantro, whole leaves only

dressing

3 tablespoons crunchy peanut butter

2 teaspoons soft light brown sugar

1 tablespoon sesame oil

1 tablespoon peanut oil

2 tablespoons rice vinegar

1 tablespoon light soy sauce

freshly squeezed juice of 1 lime

serves 4

Combine all the dressing ingredients with 125 ml/½ cup water in a bowl and stir well until the sugar has dissolved.

Heat the oil in a wok or frying pan until hot, then add the shallot, garlic and chilli. Stir-fry over high heat for 1 minute.

Add the dressing to the wok and bring to the boil, then reduce the heat and simmer gently until the dressing has thickened slightly.

When you are ready to serve the salad, put the white and red cabbage, carrot, beansprouts and coriander/cilantro in a serving bowl and pour in the warm dressing. Toss well and serve immediately.

pickled spring vegetable & marinated tofu salad

You will usually see tofu sold as soft (silken) and firm but you may also be able to buy a dark, pressed, marinated tofu. If you can't find it, it's easy enough to flavour your own with soy sauce and Chinese five-spice powder. Its creamy, mildy spiced and salty flavour goes very well with lightly-pickled spring vegetables. The vegetables are not pickled in the old-fashioned way, which leaves them limp, but kept fresh and crisp, just how mother nature intended.

12 sugar snap peas

12 mangetout/snow peas, cut in half

1 bunch of asparagus, trimmed and halved

2 tablespoons white sugar

90 ml/⅓ cup rice vinegar (or balsamic vinegar)

1 small daikon radish, cut into julienne strips

6–8 spring onions/scallions, thinly sliced on the angle

1 small bunch of fresh coriander/cilantro, chopped

3 tablespoons light soy sauce

½ teaspoon sesame oil

1 tablespoon sesame seeds, lightly toasted (optional)

marinated tofu

3 tablespoons light soy sauce

½ teaspoon Chinese five-spice powder

600-g/1¼-lbs. block firm tofu

serves 4

For the marinated tofu, put the soy sauce and five-spice powder in a bowl large enough to snugly fit the block of tofu. Add the tofu to the bowl and toss to coat in the marinade. Cover with clingfilm/plastic wrap and refrigerate for a minimum of 3 hours or overnight, turning often. Drain well and slice the tofu into thin batons.

Bring a saucepan of lightly salted water to the boil and add the sugar snaps, mangetout/snow peas and asparagus and blanche in the hot water for 1 minute. Drain and place in a large bowl of iced water until completely cold. Drain well and put into another bowl.

Put the sugar and vinegar in small saucepan and boil for 5 minutes, until thickened slightly. Remove from the heat and let cool. Pour the vinegar mix over the blanched vegetables and daikon, stir well and set aside for 30 minutes. Add the spring onions/scallions, coriander/cilantro and tofu to the pickled vegetables, gently tossing to combine. Mix the soy sauce and sesame oil in a small bowl and pour over the salad. Toss gently, then transfer to a serving dish and sprinkle the sesame seeds over the top.

Japanese garden salad with noodles

If you've never eaten a salad in a Japanese restaurant, this will be a delightful surprise. The salad itself is a simple combination of fresh ingredients plus two types of Japanese noodles – but it's the dressing that makes this so interesting.

100 g/4 oz. soba noodles

100 g/4 udon noodles

250 g/9 oz. mangetout/ snow peas

2 cos lettuce hearts or Little Gem/romaine lettuces, leaves separated

2 carrots

1 cucumber

4 ripe tomatoes

sea salt

Japanese dressing

2 tablespoons Japanese soy sauce

1½ tablespoons sugar

1½ tablespoons rice vinegar

1 tablespoon sesame oil

serves 6

Cook the soba and udon noodles separately according to the packet instructions. Drain and set aside.

Blanch the mangetout/snow peas in lightly salted, boiling water for 1 minute. Drain, refresh under cold water and dry well.

Wash and dry the lettuce leaves. Cut the carrot and cucumber into matchsticks and the tomatoes into wedges. Divide the noodles and salad ingredients between 6 serving bowls.

Put the dressing ingredients into a bowl, add 150 ml/generous ½ cup water and stir well until the sugar has dissolved. Pour over the salad and serve at once.

vermicelli salad

This aromatic vermicelli noodle salad hails from Thailand, where women regard it as a slimming aid. It is light and fresh tasting, as well as being quick and easy to prepare.

125 g/4½ oz. minced/ground pork

10 raw prawns/shrimp, shelled, deveined and coarsely chopped

½ packet (130 g/4½ oz.) thin rice vermicelli noodles

10 large dried black fungus mushrooms, soaked for about 10 minutes in cold water until soft, then coarsely chopped

1 large celery stalk, finely sliced

2 tablespoons Thai fish sauce

1 tablespoon sugar

3 tablespoons lime juice

about 6 small red chillies, finely chopped

about 6 spring onions/scallions, thinly sliced

fresh coriander/cilantro leaves, to serve

serves 4

Heat 3 tablespoons water in a saucepan, add the pork and prawns/shrimp and stir well until the meat is just cooked through.

Add the noodles, mushrooms, celery, fish sauce, sugar, lime juice, chillies and spring onions/scallions.

Stir well, transfer to a serving platter and top with coriander/cilantro leaves.

Note Vermicelli are thin rice flour noodles. They are always sold dried, but are already cooked. Soak in cold water until soft, then chop coarsely.

If the dried black fungus mushrooms are very large, they may have a small hard piece in the middle, which should be cut out and discarded.

lobster noodle salad with coconut & fruit

This delicate, exotic salad from South-east Asia makes a perfect appetizer. Fresh coconuts aren't always available, but if you see them for sale in your market, buy one and try this salad. The kind you need is the brown hairy type.

200 g/7 oz. dried beanthread noodles

2 medium cooked lobsters

2 fresh coconuts

dressing

1 tablespoon palm sugar or soft light brown sugar

freshly squeezed juice of 4 limes

1 teaspoon freshly ground green pepper

½ teaspoon sea salt

2 tablespoons peanut oil

to serve

1 fresh starfruit (carambola), thinly sliced

a small bunch of fresh coriander/cilantro leaves, coarsely chopped

a small bunch of fresh mint leaves, coarsely chopped

2 tablespoons roasted peanuts, coarsely chopped, plus extra to serve (optional)

serves 4

Put the beanthread noodles into a bowl, cover with very hot water and let soak for 10 minutes or until soft. Drain, rinse under cold running water and drain again. Chop into 5-cm/2-inch lengths with scissors and set aside.

Remove the flesh from the cooked lobsters and shred it finely.

Crack open the coconuts and scoop out the white flesh. Using a fork, shred the coconut flesh into small strips.

Put the dressing ingredients into a bowl and stir well to dissolve the sugar.

Put the noodles into a large bowl, add the lobster and coconut, pour the dressing over the top and stir gently.

Transfer to a large serving dish, arrange the starfruit slices on top, then add the coriander/cilantro, mint and peanuts. Serve extra peanuts separately, if using.

Note To crack open a coconut, wrap it in a kitchen towel. Put on a solid base, such as a clean floor, and tap it with a rolling pin.

sesame chicken & vegetable noodle salad

This recipe is typical of many with an Asian influence in that most of the sauce ingredients are simple storecupboard basics. Traditional Chinese black vinegar is substituted with balsamic vinegar here as it can be tricky to find. The fresh ingredients in this salad, such as watercress, will also not be hard to find but don't settle for anything less than a lovely, deep green, peppery bunch.

2 chicken breast fillets

175 g/6 oz. dried thin egg noodles

2 tablespoons vegetable oil

2 handfuls of fresh garlic chives, chopped into 3-cm/1¼-inch lengths

1 leek, thinly sliced

1 small red bell pepper, deseeded and thinly sliced

100 g/1 cup beansprouts

1 small bunch of watercress, leaves picked

1 tablespoon lightly toasted sesame seeds

sesame dressing

2 tablespoons sesame oil

2 tablespoons light soy sauce

1 tablespoon balsamic vinegar

1 teaspoon sugar

serves 4

Preheat the oven to 180°C (350°F) Gas 4.

To make the dressing put the sesame oil, soy sauce, vinegar and sugar in a small bowl and stir for a few seconds until the sugar has dissolved. Set aside until needed.

Put the chicken in a small roasting pan with 65 ml/¼ cup water, cover firmly with aluminium foil and cook in the preheated oven for 30 minutes. Remove from the oven and let cool. When cool enough to handle, shred the chicken and set aside until needed.

Cook the noodles in boiling water for 3 minutes. Rinse them under cold water to cool and drain well. Heat the vegetable oil in a frying pan over high heat. Add the chives, leeks and red pepper and stir-fry for 1 minute, until the vegetables have just softened. Remove the pan from the heat and stir in the beansprouts and watercress.

To serve, put the chicken, noodles and vegetables in a large bowl. Add the dressing and sesame seeds and toss well.

ginger duck salad

You would need a super-size steamer to fit a whole duck, but you can solve the space problem by cutting off the wings and keeping them for stock, and either steaming the legs separately or keeping them for another recipe.

a large bunch of fresh coriander/cilantro

7-cm/3-inch piece fresh ginger, sliced

3 garlic cloves, crushed

1 duck, legs and wings removed

125 ml/½ cup mirin, Shaohsing (rice wine) or dry sherry

100 ml/⅓ cup dark soy sauce

2 tablespoons sesame oil

2 tablespoons honey

grated zest of 1 lemon

to serve

2 bundles beanthread noodles, 30 g/1 oz. each

about 250 g/9 oz. mixed salad leaves

a handful of salted peanuts, toasted in a dry frying pan

a few sprigs of fresh coriander/cilantro

2–3 spring onions/scallions, sliced lengthways

serves 4

Wash the coriander/cilantro well, then put it into a bowl with the ginger and garlic. Mix well, then stuff into the duck cavity. Put the duck onto a large, double sheet of foil, large enough to enclose it completely. Fold the foil along the top and scrunch it closed. Fold and scrunch one end of the parcel closed.

Put a second double sheet of foil running the opposite way and scrunch closed at the sides, still keeping the end open. Put the duck, breast side down, into a large steamer with the open end upwards.

Put the mirin, soy sauce, sesame oil, honey and lemon zest into a small saucepan and heat, stirring, to dissolve the honey. Pour half the mixture into the parcel and scrunch the foil closed, making sure no liquid runs out. Reserve the remainder.

Steam over a large saucepan of water for about 1½ hours, topping up with extra boiling water as necessary. Unwrap after 1 hour and test. The duck can be slightly rare. Remove the duck from the steamer and let rest for about 10 minutes. Unwrap the foil and drain off and discard the liquid. Shred the meat from the duck and keep it warm.

Soak the noodles in hot water for 15 minutes, then drain and plunge into cold water. Drain, then toss in the reserved mirin mixture.

Arrange salad leaves on 4 plates, then add the cold noodles and shredded duck. Sprinkle with the toasted peanuts, coriander/cilantro and spring onions/scallions. Spoon the remaining dressing from the noodles over the top and serve.

accompaniments
& basic recipes

Vinegared rice

Japanese omelette

Mixed pickles

Pickled ginger

Wasabi paste

vinegared rice

Sushi is a general term for all food with *sumeshi*, or vinegared rice. Remember – sushi should never be put in the fridge (it will go hard). The vinegar will help preserve it for a few days if kept, wrapped, in a cool place, such as a shady window sill. To make sushi rice, boil 15 per cent more water than rice. Don't take the lid off during cooking or you will spoil the rice.

400 ml/1¾ cups Japanese rice*

1 piece of dried kelp (kombu), 5 cm/2 inches square, for flavouring (optional)

3 tablespoons Japanese rice vinegar

2½ tablespoons sugar

2 teaspoons sea salt

makes 1 litre/4 cups

* Please note, the rice in this recipe is measured by volume, not weight.

Put the rice in a large bowl and wash it thoroughly, changing the water several times, until the water is clear. Drain and leave in the strainer for 1 hour. If short of time, soak the rice in clear cold water for 10–15 minutes, then drain.

Transfer to a deep, heavy-based saucepan, add 460 ml/2 cups water and a piece of dried kelp (kombu), if using. Cover and bring to the boil over a high heat for about 5 minutes. Discard the kelp.

Lower the heat and simmer, covered, for about 10 minutes, or until all the water has been absorbed. Do not lift the lid. Remove from the heat and leave, still covered, for about 10–15 minutes.

Mix the rice vinegar, sugar and salt in a small jug/pitcher and stir until dissolved.

Transfer the cooked rice to a large, shallow dish or *handai* (Japanese wooden sumeshi tub). Sprinkle generously with the vinegar dressing.

Using a wooden spatula, fold the vinegar dressing into the rice. Do not stir. While folding, cool the rice quickly using a fan. Let the rice cool to body temperature before using to make sushi.

Japanese omelette

This is the basic method for cooking Japanese omelette (*tamago yaki*). In Japan it is a regular breakfast item as well as being used for sushi.

4 eggs
1 egg yolk
2½ tablespoons sugar
1 teaspoon Japanese soy sauce
sea salt
1–2 tablespoons sunflower oil

1 Japanese omelette pan or 20-cm/8-inch non-stick frying pan
hashi (chopsticks) or fork

makes 1 omelette

Using a fork, beat the eggs and egg yolk and strain through a sieve into a bowl. Add the sugar, soy sauce and a pinch of salt and stir well until the sugar has dissolved. Do not whisk or make bubbles.

Heat a Japanese omelette pan or frying pan over moderate heat and add a little oil. Spread evenly over the base by tilting the pan, then wipe off excess oil with kitchen paper, at the same time making sure the surface is absolutely smooth. Keep the oiled paper on a plate.

Lower the heat and pour one-third of the egg mixture evenly over the base by tilting the pan. If large air bubbles pop up immediately, the pan may be too hot – then remove the pan from the heat and put it back on when the egg starts to set.

Prick any air bubbles with a fork and when the egg is about to set, using chopsticks or a fork, roll the egg layer 2–3 times from one side to the other. Oil the empty base of the pan with the oiled paper and push the rolled egg back to the other side.

Again using the oiled paper, brush the base of the pan, then pour half the remaining egg mixture evenly over the base by tilting the pan and lifting the egg roll so the egg mixture flows underneath.

When the egg starts to set, roll again, using the first roll as the core. Repeat this oiling and rolling using up the remaining egg mixture. Remove from the pan and let cool before cutting.

mixed pickles

Other vegetables can be pickled and served with sushi alongside ginger. They look wonderfully colourful, adding a touch of drama to your sushi platter and making it appear very professional.

½ cucumber, about 10 cm/ 4 inches long

1 carrot, about 100 g/4 oz.

100 g/4 oz. daikon radish, peeled, or 6 red radishes

¼ small green cabbage, about 150 g/5 oz.

6 garlic cloves, finely sliced

1 tablespoon salt

½ lemon, sliced

250 ml/1 cup rice vinegar

175 g/1 cup sugar

makes about 500 ml/2 cups

Cut the cucumber in half lengthways and scoop out the seeds. Slice the cucumber, carrot and radish into very thin strips.

Slice the cabbage into 1-cm/½-inch strips. Put all the vegetables and garlic in a colander, sprinkle with salt and toss well. Set aside for 30 minutes, then rinse thoroughly and top with the sliced lemon.

Put the rice vinegar and sugar in a saucepan with 60 ml/¼ cup water. Bring to the boil, stirring until the sugar has dissolved. Boil for 5 minutes. Let cool, then pour over the vegetables and lemon. Cover and refrigerate for at least 24 hours or until needed. Keeps for 1 month in the refrigerator.

pickled ginger

The subtle flavouring of raw fish, delicate rice and fresh vegetables can easily be overpowered by the lingering flavours of previous morsels, and so ginger helps cleanse the palate.

150 g/5 oz. piece fresh ginger

1 tablespoon salt

125 ml/½ cup rice vinegar

115 g/½ cup plus 1 tablespoon sugar

1 slice fresh beetroot/beet, 1 red radish, sliced, or a drop of red food colouring (optional)

makes about 250 ml/1 cup

Peel the ginger and slice it very finely with a mandoline or vegetable peeler. Put it in a large sieve or colander and sprinkle over the salt. Set aside for 30 minutes, then rinse thoroughly.

Put the rice vinegar and sugar in a saucepan, add 60 ml/¼ cup water and bring to the boil, stirring until the sugar has dissolved. Boil for 5 minutes. Let cool, then pour over the ginger. If you would like it to be pink, like shop-bought ginger, add the beetroot/beet, radish or food colouring. Cover and refrigerate for at least 24 hours or until needed.

wasabi paste

Most of the wasabi we buy in tubes is a mixture of horseradish and wasabi – or it can be just horseradish dyed green. If you buy wasabi paste from a Japanese market, you will have a selection of various qualities, and it is always preferable to buy the best. Many Japanese cooks prefer to mix their own wasabi paste from silver-grey wasabi powder, sold in small cans, believing that the flavour is stronger and sharper. The fresh roots are not widely available, even in Japan, but if you see them in a specialist greengrocer, sold on a bed of ice, do try them. To experience the real flavour and rush of wasabi you can make your own paste from them. Traditionally grated using a sharkskin grater, a porcelain ginger grater or a very fine abrasive zester will also work. After grating, the heat in wasabi lasts for only about 10 minutes, so you must use it straight away.

wasabi from powder

1 teaspoon wasabi powder

Put the wasabi powder in a small bowl, such as an eggcup. Add 1 teaspoon water and mix with the end of a chopstick. Serve immediately.

serves 1

fresh wasabi paste

1 fresh wasabi root

a wasabi grater or ginger grater

Scrape or peel off the rough skin from the root. Using a circular motion, rub the wasabi gently against an abrasive grater onto a chopping board. Pound and chop the grated wasabi to a fine paste with a large knife or cleaver. Consume within 10 minutes.

serves 6–8

Note To keep the wasabi from discolouring for as long as possible, turn the little bowl upside down until serving – this will stop the air getting at it.

index

picture credits

Peter Cassidy Pages 1, 3, 5 above and below, 8, 10 main, 11, 12–13, 25, 26, 33, 34, 36, 38, 39, 40, 41 main, 42, 45, 46, 47, 48, 49, 50, 51, 55, 60, 63, 64, 67, 68, 70, 71, 76, 81, 91, 94, 98, 100, 108, 109, 115, 116, 118, 120, 121, **Geoff Dann** © Cico Books Pages 10 background, 41 background, 65 background, **Jeremy Hopley** Page 69, **Richard Jung** Pages 18, 58, 65 main, 75, 83, 87, 93, 99, 102, 105, 112, 113, **William Lingwood** Pages 7, 27, 56, 59, 66, 73, 74, 86, 103, 110, 114, **Diana Miller** Pages 15, 16, 17, 19, 20, 21, 23, 24, 28, 31, 32, 35, 53, 54, 61, 62, 107, 122, 125, **David Montgomery** Page 92, **William Reavell** Pages 2, 78, 79, 89, **Yuki Sugiura** Pages 5 centre, 77, 82, 85, 90, 97, **Debi Treloar** Page 72, **Pia Tryde** Page 80, **Ian Wallace** Page 106, **Kate Whitaker** Page 111

recipe credits

Nadia Arumugam Warm tossed Asian coleslaw **Kimiko Barber** Chilled somen noodles with dipping sauce, Crab noodle soup, Lobster noodle salad with coconut and fruit, Prawn and spinach wonton noodle soup, Vietnamese chicken pho **Vatcharin Bhumichitr** Sparerib and tamarind soup, Sweet and sour tofu soup, Vermicelli salad **Nicola Graimes** Vegetable and chicken ramen **Ross Dobson** Garlic and chilli rice soup with spring greens, Miso with ramen noodles & stir-fried vegetables, Pickled spring vegetable & marinated tofu salad, Sesame chicken and vegetable noodle salad, Spring chicken soup with rice noodles & herbs **Tonia George** Prawn tom yam, Salmon, soba noodle and shiitake broth, Teriyaki mackerel & shiitake noodle soup, Thai chicken, mushroom & coconut soup, Thai pork and rice soup, Vietnamese beef pho **Emi Kazuko** Egg cup sushi, Hand-moulded sushi, Japanese omelette, Lettuce boats, Mackerel sushi pieces, Simple rolled sushi, Smoked fish sushi, Stars, hearts & flowers, Step-by-step making simple rolls, Stuffed squid sushi, Vinegared rice **Elsa Petersen-Schepelern** Duck soup, Ginger duck salad, Vietnamese watercress soup **Louise Pickford** Japanese garden salad with noodles, Udon noodles with seven-spice salmon **Jennie Shapter** Sushi wraps **Fiona Smith** Introduction text, Battleship sushi, Five-colour roll, Grilled tofu roll, Inside-out avocado rolls with chives and cashews, Marinated beef sushi, Miso-marinated asparagus roll, Mixed pickles, Mushroom omelette sushi roll, Pickled ginger, Pickled salmon roll, Red miso soup with tempura croutons, Sushi balls with roast pork and pickled plums, Teriyaki chicken roll with miso dipping sauce, Wasabi mayonnaise and tuna roll, Wasabi paste, White miso soup with wakame, tofu & lettuce, Yakitori octopus roll